THE SECRET OF
GUIDANCE

THE SECRET OF GUIDANCE

By

F. B. MEYER

MOODY PRESS

CHICAGO

ISBN: 0-8024-7682-1

Printed in the United States of America

Contents

CHAPTER 1

The Secret of Guidance

MANY CHILDREN OF GOD are so deeply exercised on the matter of guidance that it may be helpful to give a few suggestions as to knowing the way in which our Father would have us walk, and the work He would have us do. The importance of the subject cannot be exaggerated; so much of our power and peace consists in knowing where God would have us be, and in being just there.

The manna only falls where the cloudy pillar broods; but it is certain to be found on the sands, which a few hours ago were glistening in the flashing light of the heavenly fire, and are now shadowed by the fleecy canopy of cloud. If we are precisely where our heavenly Father would have us to be, we are perfectly sure that He will provide food and raiment, and everything beside. When He sends His servants to Cherith, He will make even the ravens to bring them food.

How much of our Christian work has been abortive because we have persisted in initiating it for

ourselves, instead of ascertaining what God was doing, and where He required our presence! We dream
bright dreams of success. We try to command it. We
call to our aid all kinds of expedients, questionable
or otherwise. At last we turn back, disheartened and
ashamed, like children who are torn and scratched
by the brambles, and soiled by the quagmire. None
of this had come about if only we had been, from the
first, under God's unerring guidance. He might test
us, but He could not allow us to fail.

Naturally, the child of God, longing to know his
Father's will, turns to the sacred Book, and refreshes
his confidence by noticing how in all ages God has
guided those who dared to trust Him up to the very
hilt, but who at the time must have been as perplexed
as we are often now. We know how Abraham left
kindred and country, and started, with no other
guide than God, across the trackless desert to a land
which he knew not. We know how for forty years
the Israelites were led through the peninsula of Sinai,
with its labyrinths of red sandstone and its wastes of
sand. We know how Joshua, in entering the Land of
Promise, was able to cope with the difficulties of an
unknown region, and to overcome great and warlike
nations, because he looked to the Captain of the
Lord's hosts, who ever leads to victory. We know
how, in the early Church, the Apostles were enabled
to thread their way through the most difficult questions, and to solve the most perplexing problems,
laying down principles which will guide the Church

to the end of time; and this because it was revealed to them as to what they should do and say, by the Holy Spirit.

THE PROMISES FOR GUIDANCE ARE UNMISTAKABLE

Psalm 32:8: "I will instruct thee and teach thee in the way which thou shalt go." This is God's distinct assurance to those whose transgressions are forgiven, and whose sins are covered, and who are more quick to notice the least symptom of His will than horse or mule are to feel the bit.

Proverbs 3:6: "In all thy ways acknowledge Him, and He shall direct (or make plain) thy paths." A sure word, on which we may rest, if only we fulfill the previous conditions of trusting with all our heart, and of not leaning to our own understanding.

Isaiah 58:11: "The Lord shall guide thee continually." It is impossible to think that He could guide us at all if He did not guide us always. For the greatest events of life, like the huge rocking-stones in the West of England, revolve on the smallest points. A pebble may alter the flow of a stream. The growth of a grain of mustard seed may determine the rainfall of a continent. Thus we are bidden to look for a Guidance which shall embrace the whole of life in all its myriad necessities.

John 8:12: "I am the light of the world; he that followeth Me shall not walk in darkness, but shall have the light of life." The reference here seems to be to the wilderness wanderings, and the Master promises to be to all faithful souls, in their pilgrimage to the City of God, what the cloudy pillar was to the children of Israel on their march to the Land of Promise.

These are but specimens. The vault of Scripture is inlaid with thousands such, that glisten in their measure as the stars which guide the wanderer across the deep. Well may the prophet sum up the heritage of the servants of the Lord by saying of the Holy City, "All thy children shall be taught of the Lord, and great shall be the peace of thy children" (Isa. 54:13).

And yet it may appear to some tried and timid hearts as if every one mentioned in the Word of God was helped, but they are left without help. They seem to have stood before perplexing problems, face to face with life's mysteries, eagerly longing to know what to do, but no angel has come to tell them, and no iron gate has opened to them in the prison-house of circumstances.

Some lay the blame on their own stupidity. Their minds are blunt and dull. They cannot catch God's meaning, which would be clear to others. They are so nervous of doing wrong that they cannot learn clearly what is right. "Who is blind, but my servant? or deaf, as my messenger that I sent? Who is blind as he that is perfect, and blind as the Lord's servant?" Yet, how do we treat our children? One child is so bright-witted and so keen that a little hint is enough to indicate the way; another was born dull; it cannot take in your meaning quickly. Do you only let the clever one know what you want? Will you not take the other upon your knee and make clear to him the directions which baffle? Does not the distress of the tiny nursling, who longs to know that it may immediately obey, weave an almost stronger bond than that which binds you to the rest? Oh! Weary, perplexed and stupid children! Believe in the great love of God, and cast yourselves upon it, sure that He will come down to your ignorance, and suit Himself to your needs, and will take "the lambs in His arms and carry them in His bosom, and *gently lead* those that are with young" (Isa. 40:11).

There are certain practical directions which we must attend to in order that we may be led into the mind of the Lord.

OUR MOTIVES MUST BE PURE

"When thine eye is single, thy whole body is also full of light" (Luke 11:34). You have been much in darkness lately, and perhaps this passage will point up the reason. Your eye has not been single. There has been some obliquity of vision—a spiritual squint; and this has hindered you from discerning indications of God's will, which otherwise had been as clear as noonday.

We must be very careful in judging our motives, searching them as the detectives at the doors of the English House of Commons search each stranger who enters. When by the grace of God we have been delivered from grosser forms of sin, we are still liable to the subtle working of self in our holiest and loveliest hours. It poisons our motives. It breathes decay on our fairest fruit-bearing. It whispers seductive flatteries into our pleased ears. It turns the spirit from its holy purpose, as the masses of iron on ocean steamers deflect the needle of the compass from the pole.

So long as there is some thought of personal advantage, some idea of acquiring the praise and commendation of men, some aim at self-aggrandisement, it will be simply impossible to find out God's purpose concerning us. The door must be resolutely shut against all these if we would hear the still small voice. All cross-lights must be excluded if we would see the Urim and Thummim stone brighten with God's "Yes," or darken with His "No."

Ask the Holy Spirit to give you the single eye, and to inspire in your heart one aim alone: that which animated our Lord, and enabled Him to cry, as He reviewed His life, "I have glorified Thee on the earth." Let this be the watchword of our lives, "Glory to God in the highest." Then our "whole body [shall] be full of light, having no part dark, . . . as when the bright shining of a candle doth give thee light" (Luke 11:36).

OUR WILL MUST BE SURRENDERED

"My judgment is just; because I seek not Mine own will, but the will of the Father which hath sent

Me" (John 5:30). This was the secret which Jesus not only practiced, but taught. In one form or another He was constantly insisting on a surrendered will, as the key to perfect knowledge. "If any man will do His will, he shall know" (John 7:17).

There is all the difference between a will which is extinguished and one which is surrendered. God does not demand that our wills should be crushed, like the sinews of a fakir's unused arms. He only asks that they should say "Yes" to Him. Pliant to Him as the willow twig to the practiced hand.

Many a time, as the steamer has neared the bank, have I watched the little lad take his place beneath the poop, with eye and ear fixed on the captain, and waiting to shout each word he utters to the grimy engineers below; and often have I longed that my will should repeat as accurately and as promptly the words and will of God, that all the lower nature might obey.

It is for the lack of this subordination that we so often miss the guidance we seek. There is a secret controversy between our will and God's. And we shall never be right till we have let Him take, and break, and make. Oh! Do seek for that. If you cannot give, let Him take. If you are not willing, confess that you are willing to be made willing. Hand yourself over to Him to work in you, to will and to do of His own good pleasure. We must be as plastic clay, ready to take any shape that the great Potter may choose, so shall we be able to detect His guidance.

WE MUST SEEK INFORMATION FOR OUR MIND

This is certainly the next step. God has given us these wonderful faculties of brain-power, and He will not ignore them. In grace He does not cancel the action of any of His marvelous bestowments, but He uses them for the communication of His purposes and thoughts.

It is of the greatest importance, then, that we should feed our minds with facts, with reliable information, with the results of human experience, and (above all) with the teachings of the Word of God. It is matter for the utmost admiration to notice how full the Bible is of biography and history, so that there is hardly a single crisis in our lives that may not be matched from those wondrous pages. There is no book like the Bible for casting a light on the dark landings of human life.

We have no need or right to run hither and thither to ask our friends what we ought to do; but there is no harm in our taking pains to gather all reliable information, on which the flame of holy thought and consecrated purpose may feed and grow strong. It is for us ultimately to decide as God shall teach us, but His voice may come to us through the voice of sanctified common sense, acting on the materials we have collected. Of course at times God may bid us act against our reason, but these are very exceptional; and then our duty will be so clear that there can be no mistake. But for the most part God will speak in the results of deliberate consideration, weighing and balancing the *pros* and *cons*.

When Peter was shut up in prison, and could not possibly extricate himself, an angel was sent to do for him what he could not do for himself; but when they had passed through a street or two of the city, the angel left him to consider the matter for himself. Thus God treats us still. He will dictate a miraculous course by miraculous methods. But when the ordinary light of reason is adequate to the task, He will leave us to act as occasion may serve.

WE MUST BE MUCH IN PRAYER FOR GUIDANCE

The Psalms are full of earnest pleadings for clear direction: "Show me Thy way, O Lord, lead me in a plain path, because of mine enemies." It is the law of our Father's house that His children shall ask for what they want. "If any man lack wisdom, let him ask of God, who giveth to all men liberally, and upbraideth not" (James 1:5).

In a time of change and crisis, we need to be much in prayer, not only on our knees, but in that sweet form of inward prayer, in which the spirit is constantly offering itself up to God, asking to be shown His will; soliciting that it may be impressed upon its surface, as the heavenly bodies photograph themselves on prepared paper. Wrapped in prayer like this the trustful believer may tread the deck of the ocean steamer night after night, sure that He who

points the stars in their courses will not fail to direct
the soul which has no other aim than to do His will.

One good form of prayer at such a juncture is to
ask that doors may be shut, that the way be closed,
and that all enterprises which are not according to
God's will may be arrested at their very beginning.
Put the matter absolutely into God's hands from the
outset, and He will not fail to shatter the project and
defeat the aim which is not according to His holy
will.

WE MUST WAIT THE GRADUAL UNFOLDING OF GOD'S PLAN IN PROVIDENCE

God's impressions within and His Word without
are always corroborated by His Providence around,
and we should quietly wait until these three focus
into one point.

Sometimes it looks as if we are bound to act.
Everyone says we must do something; and, indeed,
things seem to have reached so desperate a pitch that
we must. Behind are the Egyptians, right and left
are inaccessible precipices; before is the sea. It is not
easy at such times to stand still and see the salvation
of God; but we must. When Saul compelled himself,
and offered sacrifice, because he thought that Samuel
was too late in coming, he made the great mistake of
his life.

God may delay to come in the guise of His Providence. There was delay ere Sennacherib's host lay

like withered leaves around the Holy City. There
was delay ere Jesus came walking on the sea in the
early dawn, or hastened to raise Lazarus. There was
delay ere the angel sped to Peter's side on the night
before his expected martyrdom. He stays long
enough to test patience of faith, but not a moment
behind the extreme hour of need. "The vision is yet
for an appointed time, but at the end it shall speak,
and shall not lie; though it tarry, wait for it, because
it will surely come; it will not tarry (Hab. 2:3).

It is very remarkable how God guides us by circumstances. At one moment the way may seem utterly blocked, and then shortly afterward some trivial
incident occurs, which might not seem much to
others, but which to the keen eye of faith speaks vol-
umes. Sometimes these signs are repeated in different ways in answer to prayer. They are not haphaz-
ard results of chance, but the opening up of circumstances in the direction in which we should walk.
And they begin to multiply, as we advance toward
our goal, just as lights do as we near a populous
town, when darting through the land by night express.

Sometimes men sigh for an angel to come to point
them their way; that simply indicates that as yet the
time has not come for them to move. If you do not
know what you ought to do, stand still until you do.
And when the time comes for action, circumstances,
like glowworms, will sparkle along your path; and

you will become so sure that you are right, when God's three witnesses concur, that you could not be surer though an angel beckoned you on.

The circumstances of our daily life are to us an infallible indication of God's will, when they concur with the inward promptings of the Spirit and with the Word of God. So long as they are stationary, wait. When you must act, they will open, and a way will be made through oceans and rivers, wastes and rocks.

We often make a great mistake, thinking that God is not guiding us at all, because we cannot see far in front. But this is not His method. He only undertakes that *the steps* of a good man should be ordered by the Lord. Not next year, but tomorrow. Not the next mile, but the next yard. Not the whole pattern, but the next stitch in the canvas. If you expect more than this you will be disappointed, and get back into the dark. But this will secure for you leading in the right way, as you will acknowledge when you review it from the hill-tops of glory.

We cannot ponder too deeply the lessons of the cloud given in the exquisite picture-lesson on Guidance (Num. 9:15-23): "And on the day that the tabernacle was reared up the cloud covered the tabernacle, namely, the tent of the testimony: and at even there was upon the tabernacle as it were the appearance of fire, until the morning. So it was alway: the cloud covered it by day, and the appearance of fire by night. And when the cloud was taken up from the tabernacle, then after that the children of Israel journeyed: and in the place where the cloud abode, there the children of Israel pitched their tents. At the commandment of the Lord the children of Israel journeyed, and at the commandment of the Lord they pitched: as long as the cloud abode upon the tabernacle they rested in their tents. And when the cloud tarried long upon the tabernacle many days, then the children of Israel kept the charge of the Lord, and journeyed not. And so it was, when the cloud was a few days upon the tabernacle; according to the commandment of the Lord they abode in their tents, and according to the commandment of the Lord they journeyed. And so it was when the cloud abode from even unto the morning, and that the cloud was taken up in the morning, then they journeyed: whether it was by day or by night that the cloud was taken up, they journeyed. Or whether it were two days, or a month, or a year, that the cloud tarried upon the tabernacle, remaining thereon, the children of Israel abode in their tents, and journeyed not; but when it was taken up, they journeyed. At the commandment of the Lord they rested in the tents and at the commandment of the Lord they journeyed: they kept the charge of the Lord at the commandment of the Lord by the hand of Moses."

Let us look high enough for guidance. Let us encourage our soul to wait only upon God till it is given. Let us cultivate that meekness which He will guide in judgment. Let us seek to be of quick under-

standing, that we may be apt to see the least sign of
His will. Let us stand with girded loins and lighted
lamps, that we may be prompt to obey. Blessed are
those servants. They shall be led by a right way to
the golden city of the saints.

Speaking for myself, after months of waiting and
prayer, I have become absolutely sure of the Guidance of my heavenly Father; and with the emphasis
of personal experience, I would encourage each troubled and perplexed soul that may read these lines to
wait patiently for the Lord, until He clearly indicates His will.

CHAPTER 2

Where Am I Wrong?

THIS IS THY EAGER QUESTION, O Christian soul, and thy bitter complaint. On the faces and in the lives of others who are known to thee, thou hast discerned a light, a joy, a power, which thou enviest with a desire which oppresses thee, but for which you should thank God devoutly. It is well when we are dissatisfied with the low levels on which we have been wont to live, and begin to ask the secret of a sweeter, nobler, more victorious life. The sleeper who turns restlessly is near awakening, and will find that already the light of the morning is shining around the couch on which slumber has been indulged too long. "Awake, thou that sleepest, and arise from the dead, and Christ shall give thee light" (Eph. 5:14).

We must, however, remember that *temperaments differ*. Some seem born in the dark, and carry with them through life an hereditary predisposition to melancholy. Their nature is set to a minor key, and responds most easily and naturally to depression. They look always on the dark side of things, and in the bluest of skies discover the cloud no bigger than a man's hand. Theirs is a shadowed pathway, where glints of sunshine strike feebly and with difficulty through the dark foliage above.

Such a temperament may be yours; and if it be, you never can expect to obtain just the same exuberant gladness which comes to others, nor must you complain if it is so. This is the burden which your Saviour's hands shaped for thee, and thou must carry it for Him, not complaining, or parading it to the gaze of others, or allowing it to master thy steadfast and resolute spirit, but bearing it silently, and glorifying God amid all. But though it may be impossible to win the joyousness which comes to others, there may at least be rest, and victory, and serenity— heaven's best gifts to man.

We must remember, also, that *emotion is no true test of our spiritual state*. Rightness of heart often shows itself in gladness of heart, just as bodily health generally reveals itself in exuberant spirits. But it is not always so. In other words, absence of joy does not always prove that the heart is wrong. It may do so, but certainly not invariably. Perhaps the nervous system may have been overtaxed, as Elijah's was in the wilderness, when, after the long strain of Carmel and his flight was over, he lay down upon the sand and asked to die—a request which God met, not with rebuke, but with food and sleep. Perhaps the Lord has withdrawn the light from the landscape in order to see whether He was loved for Himself or merely

for His gifts. Perhaps the discipline of life has cul-
minated in a Gethsemane, where the bitter cup is
being placed to the lips by a Father's hand, though
only a Judas can be seen; and in the momentary anguish caused by the effort to renounce the will, it is
only possible to lie upon the ground, with strong crying and tears, which the night wind bears to God.
Under such circumstances as these, exuberant joy is
out of place. Somber colors become the tried and
suffering soul. High spirits would be as unbecoming
here as gaiety in the home shadowed by death.
Patience, courage, faith are the suitable graces to be
manifested at such times.

But, when allowance is made for all these, it is certain that many of us are culpably missing a blessedness which would make us radiant with the light of
Paradise; and the loss is attributable to some defect
in our character which we shall do well to detect and
make right.

PERHAPS YOU DO NOT DISTINGUISH BETWEEN YOUR STANDING AND YOUR EXPERIENCE

Our experiences are fickle as April weather; now
sunshine, now cloud; lights and shadows chasing
each other over miles of heathery moor or foam-
flecked sea. But our standing in Jesus changes not.
It is like Himself—the same yesterday, today, and
forever. It did not originate in us, but in His everlasting love, which, foreseeing all that we should be,
loved us notwithstanding all. It has not been pur-

chased by us, but by His precious blood, which
pleads for us as mightily and successfully when we
can hardly claim it, as when our faith is most buoy-
ant. It is not maintained by us, but by the Holy
Spirit. If we have fled to Jesus for salvation, shelter-
ing under Him, relying on Him, and trusting Him,
though with many misgivings, as well as we may,
then we are one with Him for ever. We were one
with Him in the grave; one with Him on the Easter
morn; one with Him when He sat down at God's
right hand. We are one with Him now as He stands
in the light of His Father's smile, as the limbs of the
swimmer are one with the head, though it alone is
encircled with the warm glory of the sun, while they
are hidden beneath the waves. And no doubt or
depression can for a single moment affect or alter our
acceptance with God through the blood of Jesus,
which is an eternal fact.

You have not realized this, perhaps, but have
thought that your standing in Jesus was affected by
your changeful moods. As well might the fortune of
a wealthy heiress be diminished or increased by the
amount of her spending money. Our standing in
Jesus is our invested capital. Our emotions at the
best are but our spending money, which is ever passing through our pocket or purse, never exactly the
same. Cease to consider how you feel, and build
on the immovable rock of what Jesus is, and has
done, and is doing, and will do for you, world without end.

PERHAPS YOU LIVE TOO MUCH IN YOUR FEELINGS, TOO LITTLE IN YOUR WILL

We have no direct control over our feelings, but we have over our will. Our wills are ours, to make them God's. God does not hold us responsible for what we *feel,* but for what we *will.* In His sight we are not what we feel, but what we will. Let us, therefore, not live in the summerhouse of emotion, but in the central citadel of the will, wholly yielded and devoted to the will of God.

At the Table of the Lord, the soul is often suffused with holy emotion, the tides rise high, the tumultuous torrents of joy knock loudly against the floodgates as if to beat them down, and every element in the nature joins in the choral hymn of rapturous praise. But the morrow comes, and life has to be faced in the grimy countinghouse, the dingy shop, the noisy factory, the godless workroom; and as the soul compares the joy of yesterday with the difficulty experienced in walking humbly with the Lord, it is inclined to question whether it is quite so devoted and consecrated as it was. But, at such a time, how fair a thing it is to remark that the will has not altered its position by a hair's breadth, and to look up and say:

"My God, the spring tide of emotion has passed away like a summer brook; but in my heart of hearts, in my will, Thou knowest I am as devoted, as loyal, as desirous to be only for Thee, as in the blessed moment of unbroken retirement at Thy feet."

This is an offering with which God is well pleased. And thus we may live a calm, peaceful life.

PERHAPS YOU HAVE DISOBEYED SOME CLEAR COMMAND

Sometimes a soul comes to its spiritual adviser, speaking thus:

"I have no conscious joy, and have had but little for years."

"Did you once have it?"

"Yes, for some time after my conversion to God."

"Are you conscious of having refused obedience to some distinct command, which came into your life, but from which you shrank?"

Then the face is cast down, and the eyes film with tears, and the answer comes with difficulty:

"Yes, years ago I used to think that God required a certain thing of me; but I felt I could not do what He wished, was uneasy for some time about it, but after a while it seemed to fade from my mind, and now it does not often trouble me."

"Ah, soul, that is where you went wrong, and you will never get right till you go right back through the weary years to the point where you did drop the thread of obedience, and perform that one thing which God demanded of you so long ago, but on account of which you did leave the narrow track of implicit obedience."

Is not this the cause of depression to thousands of Christian people? They are God's children, but they are disobedient children. The Bible rings with one long demand for obedience. The key-word of the Book of Deuteronomy is, *Observe and Do*. The burden of Christ's Farewell Discourse is, *If ye love me, keep My commandments*. We must not question or reply or excuse ourselves. We must not pick and choose our way. We must not take some commands and reject others. We must not think that obedience in other directions will compensate for disobedience in some one particular. God gives one command at a time, borne in upon us, not in one way only, but in many; by this He tests us. If we obey in this, He will flood our soul with blessing, and lead us forward into new paths and pastures. But if we refuse in this we shall remain stagnant and water-logged, make no progress in Christian experience, and lack both power and joy.

PERHAPS YOU ARE PERMITTING SOME KNOWN EVIL

When water is left to stand, the particles of silt betray themselves as they fall one by one to the bottom. So if you are quiet, you may become aware of the presence in your soul of permitted evil. Dare to consider it. Do not avoid the sight as the bankrupt avoids his telltale ledgers, or as the tubercular patient the stethoscope. Compel yourself quietly to consider whatever evil the Spirit of God discovers to your soul. It may have lurked in the closets and cloisters of your being for years, suspected but unjudged. But whatever it be, and whatever its history, be sure that it has brought the shadow over your life which is your daily sorrow.

Does your will refuse to relinquish a practice or habit which is alien to the will of God?

Do you permit some secret sin to have its unhindered way in the house of your life?

Do your affections roam unrestrained after forbidden objects?

Do you cherish any resentment or hatred toward another, to whom you refuse to be reconciled?

Is there some injustice which you refuse to forgive, some charge which you refuse to pay, some wrong which you refuse to confess?

Are you allowing something yourself which you would be the first to condemn in others, but which you argue may be permitted in your own case because of certain reasons with which you attempt to smother the remonstrances of conscience?

In some cases the hindrance to conscious blessedness lies not in sins, but in *weights* which hang around the soul. Sin is that which is always and everywhere wrong; but a weight is anything which may hinder or impede the Christian life, without being positively sin. And thus a thing may be a weight to one which is not so to another. Each must be fully persuaded in his own mind. And wherever the soul is aware of its life being hindered by the presence of any one thing, then, however harmless in itself, and however innocently permitted by others, there can be no alternative, but it must be cast aside as the garments of athletes who compete for the prize in wrestling or racing.

PERHAPS YOU LOOK TOO MUCH INWARD ON SELF, INSTEAD OF OUTWARD ON THE LORD JESUS

The healthiest people do not think about their health; the weak induce disease by morbid introspection. If you begin to count your heartbeats, you will disturb the rhythmic action of the heart. If you continually imagine a pain anywhere you will produce it. And there are some true children of God who induce their own darkness by morbid self-scrutiny. They are always going back on themselves, analyzing their motives, reconsidering past acts of consecration, comparing themselves with themselves. In one form or another self is the pivot of their life, albeit that it is undoubtedly a religious life. What but darkness can result from such a course? There are certainly times in our lives when we must look within, and judge ourselves that we be not judged. But this is only done that we may turn with fuller purpose of heart to the Lord. And when once done, it needs not to be repeated. "Leaving the things behind" is the only safe motto. The question is not whether we did as well as we might, but whether we did as well as we could at the time.

We must not spend all our lives in cleaning our windows, or in considering whether they are clean, but in sunning ourselves in God's blessed light. That light will soon show us what still needs to be cleansed away, and will enable us to cleanse it with unerring accuracy. Our Lord Jesus is a perfect reservoir of everything the soul of man requires for a blessed and holy life. To make much of Him, to abide in Him, to draw from Him, to receive each moment from His fullness, is therefore the only condition of soul-health. But to be more concerned with self than with Him is like spending much time and thought over the senses of the body, and never using them for the purpose of receiving impressions from the world outside. Look off unto Jesus. "Delight thyself also in the Lord" (Ps. 37:4). "My soul, wait thou only upon God!" (Ps. 62:5).

PERHAPS YOU SPEND TOO LITTLE TIME IN COMMUNION WITH GOD THROUGH HIS WORD

It is not necessary to make long prayers, but it is essential to be much alone with God; waiting at His door; hearkening for His voice; lingering in the garden of Scripture for the coming of the Lord God in the dawn or cool of the day. No number of meetings, no fellowship with Christian friends, no amount of Christian activity can compensate for the neglect of the still hour.

When you feel least inclined for it, there is most need to make for your closet with the shut door. Do for duty's sake what you cannot do as a pleasure, and you will find it becomes delightful. You can better thrive without nourishment than become happy or strong in Christian life without fellowship with God.

When you cannot pray for yourself, begin to pray for others. When your desires flag, take the Bible in hand, and begin to turn each text into petition; or take up the tale of your mercies, and begin to translate each of them into praise. When the Bible itself becomes irksome, inquire whether you have not been spoiling your appetite by sweetmeats and renounce them; and believe that the Word is the wire along which the voice of God will certainly come to you if the heart is hushed and the attention fixed. "I will hear what God the Lord will speak" (Ps. 85:8).

More Christians than we can count are suffering from a lack of prayer and Bible study, and no revival is more to be desired than that of systematic private Bible study. There is no short and easy method of godliness which can dispense with this.

PERHAPS YOU HAVE NEVER GIVEN YOURSELF ENTIRELY OVER TO THE MASTERSHIP OF THE LORD JESUS

We are His by many ties and rights, but too few of us recognize His lordship. We are willing enough to take Him as Saviour; we hesitate to make Him King. We forget that God has exalted Him to be Prince, as well as Saviour. And the Divine order is irreversible. Those who ignore the lordship of Jesus cannot build up a strong or happy life.

Put the sun in its central throne, and all the motions of the planets assume a beautiful order. Put Jesus on the throne of the life, and all things fall into harmony and peace. Seek first the kingdom of God, and all things are yours. Consecration is the indispensable condition of blessedness.

So shall light break on thy path, such as has not shone there for many days. Yea, "thy sun shall no more go down, neither shall thy moon withdraw herself; but the Lord shall be thine everlasting light, and the days of thy mourning shall be ended" (Isa. 60: 20).

CHAPTER 3

The Secret of Christ's Indwelling

IT IS MEET that the largest church in the greatest Gentile city in the world should be dedicated to the Apostle Paul, for Gentiles are under a great obligation to him as the Apostle of the Gentiles. It is to him that we owe, under the Spirit of God, the unveiling of two great mysteries, which specially touch us as Gentiles.

The first of these, glorious as it is, we cannot now stay to discuss, though it wrought a revolution when first preached and maintained by the Apostle in the face of the most strenuous opposition. Till then, Gentiles were expected to become Jews before they were Christians, and to pass through the synagogue to the church. But he showed that this was not needful, and that Gentiles stood on the same level as Jews with respect to the privileges of the Gospel—fellow-heirs, and fellow-members of the body, and fellow-partakers of the promise in Christ Jesus through the gospel (Eph. 3:6).

The second, however, well deserves our further thought, for if only it could be realized by the children of God, they would begin to live after so Divine a fashion as to still the enemy and avenger, and to repeat in some small measure the life of Jesus on the earth.

This mystery is that *the Lord Jesus is willing to dwell within the Gentile heart.* That He should dwell in the heart of a child of Abraham was deemed a marvelous act of condescension; but that He should find a home in the heart of a Gentile was incredible. This mistake was, however, dissipated before the radiant revelation of truth made to him who, in his own judgment, was not meet to be called an Apostle, because he had persecuted the Church of God. God was pleased to make known through him "the riches of the glory of this mystery among the Gentiles; which is CHRIST IN YOU, the hope of glory" (Col. 1:27).

"Master, where dwellest Thou?" they asked of old. And in reply Jesus led them from the crowded Jordan bank to the slight tabernacle of woven osiers where He temporarily lodged. But if we address the same question to Him now, He will point, not to the high and lofty dome of heaven, not to the splendid structure of stone or marble, but to the happy spirit that loves, trusts, and obeys Him. "Behold," saith He, "I stand at the door and knock. If any man hear My voice, and open the door, I will come in to him." "We will come," He said, including His Father with Himself, "and make our abode with him." He promised to be within each believer as a tenant in a house;

THE SECRET OF CHRIST'S INDWELLING

as sap in the branch; as lifeblood and life-energy in
each member, however feeble, of the body.

THE MYSTERY

Christ is in the believer. He indwells the heart by
faith, as the sun indwells the lowliest flowers that un-
furl their petals and bare their hearts to its beams.
Not because we are good. Not because we are trying
to be wholehearted in our consecration. Not because
we keep Him by the tenacity of our love. But because we believe, and in believing, have thrown open
all the doors and windows of our nature. And He
has come in.

He probably came in so quietly that we failed to
detect His entrance. There was no footfall along the
passage. The chime of the golden bells at the foot of
His priestly robe did not betray Him. He stole in on
the wing of the morning, or like the noiselessness
with which nature arises from her winter's sleep and
arrays herself in the robes which her Creator has prepared for her. But this is the way of Christ. He does
not strive, nor cry, nor lift up nor cause His voice to
be heard. His tread is so light that it does not break
bruised reeds. His breath so soft that it can reillu-
mine dying sparks. Do not be surprised, therefore,
if you cannot tell the day or the hour when the Son
of Man came to dwell within you. Only know that
He has come. "Know ye not as to your own selves,
that Jesus Christ is in you, unless ye be reprobate?"
(2 Cor. 13:5)

It is very wonderful. Yes; the heavens, even the Heavens of heavens, with all their light and glory, alone seem worthy of Him. But even there He is not more at home than He is with the humble and contrite spirit that simply trusts in Him. In His early life, He said that the Father dwelt in Him so really that the words He spake and the works He did were not His own, but His Father's. And He desires to be in us as His Father was in Him, so that the outgoings of our life may be channels through which He, hidden within, may pour Himself forth upon men.

It is not generally recognized. It is not; though that does not disprove it. We fail to recognize many things in ourselves and in nature around, which are nevertheless true. But there is a reason why many whose natures are certainly the temple of Christ, remain ignorant of the presence of the wonderful Tenant that sojourns within. *He dwells so deep.* Below the life of the body, which is as the curtain of the tent; below the life of the soul, where thought and feeling, judgment and imagination, hope and love, go to and fro, ministering as white-stoled priests in the holy place; below the play of light and shade, resolution and will, memory and hope, the perpetual ebb and flow of the tides of self-consciousness, there, through the Holy Spirit Christ dwells, as of old the Shekinah dwelt in the Most Holy Place, closely shrouded from the view of man.

It is comparatively seldom that we go into these deeper departments of our being. We are content to live the superficial life of sense. We eat, we drink, we sleep. We give ourselves to enjoy the lust of the flesh, the lust of the eyes, and the pride of life. We fulfill the desires of the flesh and of the mind. Or we abandon ourselves to the pursuit of knowledge and culture, of science and art. We make short incursions into the realm of morals, that sense of right and wrong which is part of the makeup of men. But we have too slight an acquaintance with the deeper and more mysterious chamber of the spirit. Now this is why the majority of believers are so insensible of their Divine and wonderful Resident, who makes the regenerated spirit His abode.

It is to be accepted by faith. We repeat here our constant mistake about the things of God. We try to feel them. If we feel them, we believe them; otherwise we take no account of them. We reverse the Divine order. We say, feeling, FAITH, FACT. God says FACT, FAITH, *feeling.* With Him feeling is of small account—He only asks us to be willing to accept His own Word, and to cling to it because He has spoken it, in entire disregard of what we may feel.

I am distinctly told that Christ, though He is on the Throne in His ascended glory, is also within me by the Holy Ghost. I confess I do not feel Him there. Often amid the assault of temptation or the fury of the storm that sweeps over the surface of my nature, I cannot detect His form or hear Him say, "It is I." But I dare to believe He is there; not without me, but within; not as a transient sojourner for a night,

but as a perpetual inmate; not altered by my changes
from earnestness to lethargy, from the summer of
love to the winter of despondency, but always and
unchangeably the same. And I say again and again,
"Jesus, Thou art here. I am not worthy that Thou
shouldest abide under my roof; but Thou hast come.
Assert Thyself. Put down all rule, and authority,
and power. Come out of Thy secret chamber, and
possess all that is within me, that it may bless Thy
holy name."

Catherine of Siena at one time spent three days in
a solitary retreat, praying for a greater fullness and
joy of the Divine presence. Instead of this, it seemed
as though legions of wicked spirits assailed her
with blasphemous thoughts and evil suggestions. At
length, a great light appeared to descend from above.
The devils fled, and the Lord Jesus conversed with
her. Catherine asked Him:

"Lord, where wert Thou when my heart was so
tormented?"

"I was in thy heart," He answered.

"O Lord, Thou art everlasting truth," she replied,
"and I humbly bow before Thy word; but how can
I believe that Thou wast in my heart when it was
filled with such detestable thoughts?"

"Did these thoughts give thee pleasure or pain?"
He asked.

"An exceeding pain and sadness," was her reply.

To whom the Lord said, "Thou wast in woe and
sadness because I was in the midst of thy heart. My

presence it was which rendered those thoughts insupportable to thee. When the period I had determined for the duration of the combat had elapsed, I sent forth the beams of My light, and the shades of hell were dispelled, because they cannot resist that light."

THE GLORY OF THIS MYSTERY

When God's secrets break open, they do so in glory. The wealth of the root hidden in the ground is revealed in the hues of orchid or scent of rose. The hidden beauty of a beam of light is unraveled in the sevenfold color of the rainbow. The swarming, infinitesimal life of southern seas breaks into waves of phosphorescence when cleft by the keel of the ship. And whenever the unseen world has revealed itself to mortal eyes, it has been in glory. It was especially so at the Transfiguration, when the Lord's nature broke from the strong restraint within which He confined it and revealed itself to the eye of man. "His face did shine as the sun, and His garments became white as the light" (Matthew 17:2, ASV).

So when we accept the fact of His existence within us deeper than our own, and make it one of the aims of our life to draw on it and develop it, we shall be conscious of a glory transfiguring our life and irradiating ordinary things, such as will make earth, with its commonest engagements, like as the vestibule of Heaven.

The wife of Jonathan Edwards had been the subject of great fluctuations in religious experience and

frequent depression, till she came to the point of re-
nouncing the world, and yielding herself up to be
possessed by these mighty truths. But so soon as this
was the case, a marvelous change took place. She
began to experience a constant, uninterrupted rest;
sweet peace and serenity of soul; a continual rejoic-
ing in all the works of God's hands, whether of nature or of daily providence; a wonderful access to
God by prayer, as it were seeing Him and immediately conversing with Him; all tears wiped away; all
former troubles and sorrows of life forgotten, ex-
cepting grief for past sins and for the dishonor done
to Christ in the world; a daily sensible doing and
suffering everything for God, and doing all with a
continual uninterrupted cheerfulness, peace and joy.

Such glory—the certain pledge of the glory to be
revealed—is within reach of each reader of these
lines who will dare day by day to reckon that Christ
lives within, and will be content to die to the energies
and promptings for the self-life so that there may be
room for the Christ-life to reveal itself. "I have been
crucified," said the greatest human teacher of this
Divine art; "Christ liveth in me; I live by faith in the
Son of God" (Gal. 2:20).

THE RICHES OF THE GLORY OF THIS MYSTERY

When this mystery or secret of the Divine life in
man is apprehended and made use of, it gives great
wealth to life. If all the treasures of wisdom, knowledge, power, and grace reside in Jesus, and He is

become the cherished and honored resident of our nature, it is clear that we also must be greatly enriched. It is like a poor man having a millionaire friend come to live with him.

There are riches of patience. Life is not easy to any of us. No branch escapes the pruning knife; no jewel the wheel; no child the rod. People tyrannize over and vex us almost beyond endurance. Circumstances strain us till the chords of our hearts threaten to snap. Our nervous system is overtaxed by the rush and competition of our times. Indeed, we have need of patience!

Never to relax the self-watch; never to indulge in unkind or thoughtless criticism of others; never to utter the hasty word, or permit the sharp retort; never to complain except to God; never to permit hard and distrustful thoughts to lodge within the soul; to be always more thoughtful of others than self; to detect the one blue spot in the clouded sky; to be on the alert to find an excuse for those who are forward and awkward, to suffer the aches and pains, the privations and trials of life, sweetly, submissively, trustfully; to drink the bitter cup, with the eye fixed on the Father's face, without a murmur or complaint:—this needs patience, which mere stoicism could never give.

And we cannot live such a life till we have learned to avail ourselves of the riches of the indwelling Christ. The beloved Apostle speaks of being a partaker of the patience which is in Jesus (Rev. 1:9).

So may we be. That calm, unmurmuring, unreviling patience, which made the Lamb of God dumb before His shearers, is ours.

Robert Hall was once overheard saying amid the heat of an argument, "Calm me, O Lamb of God!"

But we may go further and say, "Lord Jesus, let Thy patience arise in me, as a spring of fresh water in a briny sea."

There are riches of grace. Alone among the great cities of the world, Jerusalem had no river. But the glorious Lord was in the midst of her, and He became a place of broad rivers and streams, supplying from Himself all that rivers gave to cities, at the foot of whose walls the welcome waters lapped (Isa. 33: 21).

This is a picture of what we have, who dare to reckon on the indwelling of our glorious Lord, as King, Lawgiver, and Saviour. He makes all grace to abound toward us, so that we have a sufficiency for all emergencies, and can abound in every good work. In His strength, ever rising up within us, we are able to do as much as those who are dowered with the greatest mental and natural gifts, and we escape the temptations to vainglory and pride by which they are beset.

The grace of purity and self-control, of fervent prayer and understanding in the Scriptures, of love for men and zeal for God, of lowliness and meekness, of gentleness and goodness—all is in Christ; and if Christ is in us, all is ours also. O that we would dare to believe it, and draw on it, letting down the pitcher of faith into the deep well of Christ's indwelling, opened within us by the Holy Ghost!

It is impossible, in these brief limits, to elaborate further this wonderful thought. But if only we would meet every call, difficulty, and trial, *not* saying, as we so often do, "I shall never be able to go through it," but saying, "I cannot; but Christ is in me, and He can," we should find that all trials were intended to reveal and unfold the wealth hidden within us, until Christ was literally formed within us, and His life manifested in our mortal body (2 Cor. 4:10).

1. Be still each day for a short time, sitting before God in meditation, and ask the Holy Spirit to reveal to you the truth of Christ's indwelling. Ask God to be pleased to make known to *you* what is the riches of the glory of this mystery (Col. 1:27).

2. Reverence your nature as the temple of the indwelling Lord. As the Easterner bares his feet, and the Westerner his head, on entering the limits of a temple, so be very careful of aught that would defile the body or soil the soul. No beasts must herd in the temple courts. Get Christ to drive them out. "Know ye not that ye are a temple of God? The temple of God is holy, and such are ye."

3. Hate your own life. "If any man hateth not his own life," said our Lord, "he cannot be My disciple" (Luke 14:26). And the word translated "life" is *soul,* the seat and center of the self-life with its restless energies and activities, its choices and decisions,

its ceaseless strivings at independence and leadership. This is the greatest hindrance to our enjoyment of the indwelling Christ. If we will acquire the habit of saying "No," not only to our bad but our good self; if we will daily deliver ourselves up to death for Jesus' sake; if we will take up our cross and follow the Master, though it be to His grave, we shall become increasingly conscious of being possessed by a richer, deeper, Diviner life than our own.

CHAPTER 4

Fact! Faith! Feeling!

THESE THREE WORDS stand for three most important factors in character and life. We all have to do with them in one form or another, but it is above all things necessary that we should place them in the right order.

Most people try to put *Feeling* first, with as much success as if they tried to build the top story of a house before laying its foundations. Their order is—

FEELING,		FEELING,
FACT,	or	FAITH,
FAITH.		FACT.

Others seek *Faith* first, without considering the Facts on which alone Faith and Feeling can rest. They resemble the man, who desiring to get warm on a frosty night, refuses to approach the fire which burns brightly on the hearth.

The only possible order that will bring blessing and comfort to the heart is that indicated in our title:—

God's *Facts,* laid like a foundation of adamant.
Our *Faith,* apprehending and resting on them.

Joyous *Feelings,* coming, it may be at once, or
after the lapse of days and months, as God will.

FACT

The facts of which we are told in the Bible are
like steppingstones across a brook. Before you reach
the shallows where they lie, you wonder how you will
get over, but on stepping down to the margin of the
water, they span the space from bank to bank. When
you have reached one you can step to another, and
so across. It is absurd to consult feeling, or look for
faith, while still at a distance from the brookside, or
if you persist in going above or below that primitive
bridge of stones. You must come down to them,
consider them, see how strongly fixed they are in the
oozy bed, notice how easily the villagers pass and
repass; *then* you will feel able to trust them, and
finally, with a light heart and great sense of relief,
step from one to another.

Let us recall a few facts which may help us first to
faith, and then to feeling.

*It is a fact that God loves each of us with the ten-
derest and most particular love.* You may not believe or feel it; the warm summer sun may be shining
against your shuttered and curtained window without making itself seen or felt within; but your failure
to realize and appreciate the fact of God's love toward you cannot alter its being so.

It is a fact that in Jesus every obstacle has been removed out of the way of your immediate forgiveness and acceptance. God was in the dying Saviour, putting away sin, bearing our sins in His own body on the tree, reconciling the world to Himself. You may not believe this, or feel the joy of it, but that does not alter the fact that it is so.

After the peace was signed between the North and the South, ending the Civil War, there were soldiers hiding in the woods, starving on berries, who might have returned to their homes. They either did not know, or did not credit, the good news, and they went on starving long after their comrades had been welcomed by their wives and children. Theirs was the loss, but their failure in knowledge or belief did not alter the fact that peace was proclaimed and that the door was wide open for their return.

A friend may have paid all my debts in my native village, from which I have fled, fearing arrest and disgrace. He may have done it so speedily that my credit has never been impaired, or my good name forfeited. There may be all the old love and honor waiting to greet me. He may have told me so; but if I still absent myself, and refuse to return, my folly in this respect cannot undo those beneficent acts, though it perpetuates my misery.

It is a fact that the moment a soul trusts Christ, he is born into God's family and becomes a child. There is no doubt about this. You may not feel good, or earnest, or anxious; you may even be conscious of

recent failure; you may be spending your days under
a pall of somber depression; but if you have received
Christ, and have truly trusted in Him, you have been
born again, not of man, or of the will of the flesh, but
of God (John 1:12). You may be a prodigal or inconsistent child, but you are a child. If you were
wise you would take the child's place at the Father's
table, and enjoy His smile. They await you. But if
you still remain out in the cold, as the elder brother
in the parable, you do not alter the fact that your
place is ready for you to occupy when you will.

*It is a fact that God takes what we give, and as
soon as we give it.* There is no long interval. When
we let go, He receives. When we place ourselves on
His altar, we are immediately sealed as His. When
we consecrate ourselves, He accepts. The divine act
is instantaneous. You may not be aware of this, and
continue giving yourself day after day. If you do,
you burden yourself with needless anxiety; you continue offering what is not now yours to give, and you
lose the blessedness of realizing what it is to be the
absolute property, chattel and slave of the blessed
Master; but your mistake cannot alter the fact that
God took you at your word when first you made
yourself over to Him in a solemn act of dedication.
Shall our want of faith make of none effect the
faithfulness of God?

*It is a fact that in Jesus Christ we are seated in
heavenly places.* We cannot alter this. We may not

believe it, or avail ourselves of all the privileges
which it implies, or enjoy the blessedness of nearness
to Jesus; but such is, nevertheless, our rightful position in the divine order. If we are united with Jesus
by the slenderest strand of faith, we are as much one
with Him as the loftiest saints; and where the Head
is, there is also the Body. In Him we died on the
cross, and so met the righteous demands of the holy
law. In Him we lay in the grave, and so passed out
of the region ruled by the Prince of the Power of the
air. In Him we rose and ascended far above all might
and dominion, principality and power.

Is Satan under Christ's feet? In God's purpose he
is under ours also. Are death and the grave for ever
behind Christ? So, in God's purpose, we have passed
to the Easter side of them both, and are to the wind-
ward of the storm. As far as their sting or terror is
concerned they are like the Egyptians dead on the
sea shore. Has the great High Priest passed through
the heavens within the veil? So, in the purpose of
God, we too have passed from the outer court into
the Holy Place, where we offer gifts, sacrifices, sup-
plications, and intercessions for all men.

All this may appear unreal and impossible, as the
idea of being the bride of a prince to a poor Cinder-
ella, but is nevertheless our true position. These are
the facts of the eternal world, whether you avail yourself of them or not. There are not a few cases on
record of slaves starving in bondage because they

would not avail themselves of freedom; and of noble-
men living a hard and difficult life because they
would not claim their rights!

*It is a fact that there is a share in the gift of Pente-
cost waiting for each member of Christ.* He received
gifts even for the rebellious. To each grace has been
given. The promise of the Holy Ghost is to as many
as the Lord our God shall call. Without doubt you
have a share in that infilling, that divine unction, that
marvelous power in service, which transformed the
apostles from being timid sheep to lions in fight. You
may never have put in your claim, but there is no
grace that others have which you may not obtain.
All things are yours. God has made over to you the
unsearchable riches of Christ. Eye hath not seen,
nor ear heard, nor the heart of man conceived, all
the stores of grace and love and power which are
yours in Christ, accumulating for you in the Divine
Deposit Bank. It seems a thousand pities that you
should live a beggar's life when such wealth and
power are yours; but if you persist in doing so, your
folly and blindness do not alter the fact that the fullness of God is yours in Christ.

These are some of those facts, made known to us
in the Word of God, which will conduct us over the
brook of turbid emotion to firm standing ground. Let
us give up worrying about our faith, or feeling the
pulse of emotion, and come to rest on them, assured
that they are more stable than heaven or earth.

FAITH

If you want a true faith, do not think about it, but look away to the facts of which we have been speaking. We find no difficulty in trusting our friends, because we open our hearts, like south windows, to their love. We recall all their interpositions in our behalf. We remember all they have promised and performed. Where would be our difficulty about faith if we ceased worrying about it, and were occupied with the object of faith—Jesus Christ our Lord?

Faith is more than Creed. In a creed we believe *about* a person or circumstance; but in faith we repose our trust *upon* a person. We must not believe about Christ only, but in Him, as Livingstone did, when on one occasion he was opposed at nightfall by an army of infuriated savages, and was tempted to steal away in the dark; but his eye lit on the promise, "I will be with you all the days," and he wrote, "I went to sleep because I knew it was the word of a perfect gentleman." Do not believe about Christ, but in Him.

Faith concerns itself with a person. We are saved and blessed by the faith that passes through the facts of our Saviour's life to Himself. We rest not on the atonement, but on Him who made it; not on the death, but on Him who died; not on the resurrection, but on Him who rose, ascended, and ever liveth to make intercession; not in statements about Him, but in Him of whom they are made.

Many a time the question is asked by the inquirer, "Have I the right kind of faith?" It is a needful question, because there is a dead and spurious faith which will fail us in the supreme crisis, as the badly-canned meats did the Arctic exploration party, who on returning to their heap of stores, found them useless, and starved.

There is one simple reply, "All faith that turns towards Jesus is the right faith." It may bring no conscious rapture. It may be as weak as the woman's touch on His garment's hem. It may be small and insignificant as a grain of mustard seed. It may be despairful as Peter's cry, "Lord, save, or I perish!" But if its deepest yearning be Christ—Christ—Christ, it is the tiny thread which will bring the lost soul through subterranean passages, in which it had been well-nigh overwhelmed, into the light of life.

True Faith reckons on God's Faith. In earlier life I used to seek after greater faith by considering how great God was, how rich, how strong; why should He not give me money for His work, since He was so rich? Why not carry the entire burden of my responsibilities, since He was so mighty? These considerations helped me less, however, than my now certain conviction that He is absolutely faithful; faithful to His covenant engagements in Christ, faithful to His promises, and faithful to the soul that at His clear call has stepped out into any enterprise for Him. We may lose heart and hope, our head may turn dizzy and our heart faint, lover and friend may stand at a distance, the mocking voices of our foes suggest that God has forgotten or forsaken; but He abideth faithful, He cannot deny Himself, He cannot disown the helpless child whom He has begotten, because it ails, He cannot throw aside responsibilities He has assumed. He has made, and He must bear.

Oftentimes I have gone to God in dire need, aggravated by nervous depression and heart-sickness, and said, "My faith is flickering out. Its hand seems paralyzed, its eye blinded, its old glad song silenced forever. But Thou art faithful, and I am reckoning on Thee!" The soul loves to go behind the promises of God to Himself who made them, as the wife needs not quote the pledges made by her husband in the marriage-service when she is sure of him, and feels the pressure of his hand.

Do not trouble about your Faith; reckon on God's Faithfulness. If He bids you step out on the water, He knows that He can bring you safely back to the boat. When an Alpine guide takes you over a ragged piece of ice, he considers whether, in the event of your utter collapse, he is not able to carry you through by the strength of his iron grasp and sinewy frame. What iron is to the blood, that the thought of God's faithfulness is to faith. "Sarah . . . received power . . . since she counted him faithful who had promised" (Heb. 11:11, ASV); Abraham "waxed strong through faith, giving glory to God" (Rom. 4:20, ASV).

Faith bears Fruit. It cannot help it, because it

links the soul with Christ, so that the energy of His life pours into it through the artery of faith, and, as it comes in, so it must make a way for itself out. Fruit is (so to speak) forced from the believing soul. Why does the lark sing? It cannot help it, because the spirit of spring has been poured into its heart. Why does the branch bear fruit? It cannot help it, because the life-forces are ever pouring up from the root. Why does a child run to meet its mother? It cannot help it, because its heart has imbibed her nature. So the believer, united to Christ, receives grace upon grace from His heart, and from the abundance of His indwelling his life speaks.

It is not difficult to obtain faith like this. Put your will on the side of Christ—not a passing wish, but the whole desire and choice of your being. Be willing to believe; or be willing to be made willing to believe. Lift your eyes toward Christ. If you cannot see Him, look toward the place where you think He is. Remind Him that He is the Author of faith, and that it is His gift. Claim it from Him, and reckon that in answer to your appeal He does confer this priceless boon. You may not feel faith, but you will find yourself unconsciously thinking of Christ, counting on Christ, going out toward Christ; and that engagement of the soul with Christ is faith.

Be careful of the tender plant which has thus been planted within you. Give it plenty of sunshine. Live outside yourself in the consideration of what Christ is. Feed faith on her native food of promise, and let her breathe her native air on the hills of communion. Treat all suggestions of doubt as you would questions as to the fidelity of your dearest friend. Avoid the cold blast that sets in from skeptical books and talk. Be sure to live up to your highest conceptions of duty toward God and man. Your faith will be in exact proportion to your obedience. Inability to trust almost always denotes some failure to obey. If faith is faltering, ask yourself whether you have not dropped the thread of obedience, and go back to the place where you lost it. Christian could not face the lions till he had sorrowfully retraced his steps to the arbor where he slept and had recovered his roll.

Faith is pre-eminently the receptive faculty. It not only reckons that God gives, but it stretches out its hand to take. "As many as *received* him, to them gave he power to become the sons of God, even to them that *believe* on his name" (John 1:12). We receive the at-one-ment from the Lord who died, and we receive the abundance of God's grace from the Lord who ever lives, so that we reign in this mortal life as we hope to reign when the heavens and earth have fled away, and there is no more sea to divide us from our beloved (Rom. 8:17). The beautiful garments are prepared, faith arrays herself in them. The armor hangs on the wall, faith girds herself in it. The water of life gushes at her feet, but faith catches it up, as did Gideon's three hundred men. Faith thus deals definitely with God. She does not simply see His gifts as the passer-by the jewels in the shop window, but she knows that all the regalia of God's kingdom are hers, and she takes them as she will. She hears the voice of her Father saying: "Thou art ever with Me, and all that I have is thine."

It was not enough that God should give the land of Canaan by promise and covenant to the chosen race. They had to go in to possess it, to put their foot down on its soil, to till its acres, and to live in its rich products. So it must be with the believer. He is first united with Jesus by a living faith, which *rests* in Him as Saviour, Friend, and King; then he reckons that the Son of God is well able to make him His joint-heir of all His boundless wealth, and, lastly, he learns the art of receiving and using the plenteous heritage, and year by year presses the fences of his possession farther back, taking in more and more of that vast extent of territory which has been assigned to him in Jesus.

Oh! Settler on the boundless continent of God's fullness in Jesus, get thee up into the high mountain. Look northward, southward, eastward and westward, over the lengths, and breadths, and depths, and heights of the love of God. It is all yours from the river of Time which rises at your foot to the utmost sea of Eternity. Be not slack to go up and possess the land, and to inherit all which God has freely bestowed on you in the Son of His love.

FEELING

Our feelings are very deceptive, because so easily

wrought on from without. They are affected by the state of our health, changes in the weather, the society or absence of those who love. When the air is light, and the sun shines, and we have slept well, we are more likely to feel disposed toward God than when the dripping November fog drenches the woodlands. The Father who made us and knows our frame, understands this; so much so, that when Elijah, after the strain of Carmel, his swift flight, and his disappointment at Jezebel's continued obduracy, threw himself beneath the juniper tree and asked for a swift death, God sent him sleep for his exhausted nervous system, and food for his hunger.

As a rule, Faith fruits in Feeling. "Being justified by faith, we have peace with God . . . and not only so, but we joy in God, through our Lord Jesus Christ." "Believing we rejoice with joy unspeakable, and full of glory." When the prodigal returned, the father bade them slay the fatted calf, saying: "Let us eat and be merry." There is relief from a heavy burden of sin, the ectasy of pardon, the light of the Father's face, the sense of rightness, the calm outlook on the future. When the King comes to His own the bells ring out their peals on the waiting air, as though intoxicated with delight.

Happy and blessed feeling is the effect of the Spirit's work on the soul. "The fruit of the Spirit is love, joy, peace . . ." He is the earnest of our inheritance, and though in our minority we cannot expect to enter on the fullness of our heritage, we

are privileged to enjoy its firstfruits. There are pre-
libations of the river of His pleasures, and stray notes
from the full chorus of bliss. When the Holy Ghost
reveals the Bridegroom, the loving heart is glad, even
though the nuptials are not yet celebrated.

*But the lack of feeling does not always indicate we
are wrong.* There may be causes, as we have seen,
which account for our depression. It may be that
Christ would teach us to distinguish between love
and the emotion of love, between joy and the rapture of joy, between peace and the sense of peace. Or
perhaps He may desire to ascertain whether we cling
to Him for Himself or for His gifts.

Children greet their father from the window, as he
turns the corner and comes down the street. He
hears the rush of their feet along the hall as he in-
serts his key in the door. But one day he begins to
question whether they greet him for the love they
bear him or for the gifts with which he never forgets
to fill his pockets. One day, therefore, he gives them
due notice that there will be no gifts when he returns
at night. Their faces fall, but when the hour of return arrives they are at the window as usual, and
there is the same tramping of little feet to the door.
"Ah," he says, "my children love me for myself,"
and he is glad.

Our Father sometimes cuts off the supply of joy,
and suffers us to hunger, that He may know what is
in our hearts, and whether we love Him for Himself.
If we still cling to Him as Job did, He is glad, and

restores comforts to His mourners with both hands.

Seek feeling, and you will miss it; be content to live without it, and you will have all you require. If you are always noticing your heart-beats, you will bring on heart disease. If you are always muffling against cold, you will become very subject to chills. If you are perpetually thinking about your health, you will induce disease. If you are always consulting your feelings, you will live in a dry and thirsty land, where no water is. He that saveth his soul shall lose it.

Be indifferent to emotion. If it is there, be thankful; if it is absent, go on doing the will of God, reckoning on Him, speaking well of Him behind His back, and, above all, giving no signs of what you are suffering, lest you be a stumbling block to others. Then joy will overtake you as a flood. He will make you sit at His table, and gird Himself to come forth and serve you.

CAUTIONS

There are five concluding cautions for the culture of the devout life, attention to which will generally result in holy joy and peace.

1. *We must be still before God.* The life around us, in this age, is preeminently one of rush and effort. It is the age of the express-train and telegraph. Years are crowded into months, and weeks into days. This feverish haste threatens the religious life. The stream has already entered our churches, and stirred

their quiet pools. Meetings crowd on meetings. The same energetic souls are found at them all, and engaged in many good works beside. But we must beware that we do not substitute the active for the contemplative, the valley for the mountaintop. Neither can with safety be divorced from the other. The sheep must go in and out. The blood must come back to the heart to be recharged, and fitted to be impelled again to the extremities.

We must make time to be alone with God. The closet and the shut door are indispensable. We must lose the glare of the sunny piazza that we may see the calm angel-figures bending above the altar. We must escape the din of the world, to become accustomed to the accents of the still, small voice. Like David, we must sit before the Lord. Happy are they who have an observatory in their heart-house to which they can often retire beneath the great arch of Eternity, turning their telescope to the mighty constellations that turn beyond life's fever, and reaching regions where the breath of human applause or censure cannot follow!

It is only in such moments that the best spiritual gifts will loom in our vision, or we shall have grace to receive them It is impossible to rush into God's presence, catch up anything we fancy, and run off with it. To attempt this will end in mere delusion and disappointment. Nature will not unveil her rarest beauty to the chance tourist. Pictures which are the result of a life of work do not disclose their secret loveliness to the saunterer down a gallery. No charter can be read at a glance. And God's best can not be ours apart from patient waiting in His Holy Presence. The superficial may be put off with a parable, a pretty story, but it is not given such to know the mysteries of the Kingdom of Heaven.

2. *We must be possessed by an eager desire.* There is a difference between wishing for a thing and willing it. In a single hour we may wish for a hundred differing objects, and forget them. But how different from this is the fixed determination, the settled purpose of the *will!*

The lad catches sight of some equipment for his sport, the student of a precious book, the lover of a rare and jeweled ornament which he covets for the one he loves—and in each case the will is wrought upon till it resolves to acquire at any cost. Then privation and self-sacrifice and delay are cheerfully encountered. Nothing can extinguish or slacken the determination that follows hard after its quest. So with us. We must hunger and thirst; we must be possessed by strong and passionate desire; we must be resolved even to use violence to take the Kingdom of Heaven. The expressions of Scripture are all so intense—the heart pants for the waterbrooks; Jacob will not let the angel go; the widow troubles the unjust judge day and night. We too may have this strong desire if we will let the Spirit of God produce it within our hearts. But the merchantman must be bent on seeking and finding the goodly pearl. We must strive to enter the strait gate. We must agonize (to use the Apostle's word) as the athlete for the crown.

3. *We must have a promise in our hand.* This is the true method of dealing with God. Search the Bible for some holy word which exactly fits your case. It will not be hard to find one, since it abounds with personal incidents, culled from every conceivable variety of life. Then, when it has been discovered, and perhaps borne in on you by the divine Spirit, take it with you into the presence of God, or place your finger upon it as you pass into the presence-chamber with hushed and reverent step. The promises are our inventory of possession, and our need should make us look up for and claim the blessing intended to meet it.

CHAPTER 5

Why Sign the Pledge?

THE FEELING among Christians against strong drink is growing. By the efforts and self-sacrifice of tens of thousands, a strong public sentiment can be formed, like a mighty breakwater. An arrest may be placed on the onward march of drunkenness, and many a bark, battered by the fury of Passion and Self-indulgence, safely moored in the haven, sheltered from utter ruin, and able to repair its terrible wreckage. Let us do our best to build our few stones into this great breakwater, which is only made up by the small work of unknown and soon-forgotten builders.

One important means by which so much can be done, is the use of the Pledge. It will be a great mistake if the signing of the Pledge should ever fall into disuse, or become an object of contempt.

1. *Reckon on God.* If you desire spiritual gifts, not for your own gratification, but for the glory of Christ; if so far as you know, your heart is rid of evil, and your life of sinful habit; if you perceive that the promise is for you, because you are not only

a son, but an heir of God, and a joint-heir with
Christ; if you feel an eager desire that God has in-
stilled to lead you to this very point—*then* open your
mouth wide, and believe that God fills it; unshutter
every window, and believe that the light enters;
throw wide every aperture, and believe that you have
received what you needed and sought. According to
your faith, it shall be unto you.

In some moment of need, or when you least expect it, or when engaged in usual toils, some glad
consciousness of joy, or peace, or nearness to Christ,
or power over others, will be the evidence that you
did receive.

2. *We must care for others.* No life can be blessed
which is self-centered, and shut in, as the Dead Sea,
by giant walls. The secret of having is giving; of
learning is teaching; of climbing to the throne is by
stooping to wash the feet of the disciples. Think
more of others than yourself, and your own life shall
be never so rich and prosperous. "I want—I want—
Christians to go all over the world, and spread the
Gospel." These words, spoken with labored breath,
were almost the last uttered by a beloved Christian
worker.

And yet in some quarters there is a disposition to
think and speak lightly of the Pledge.

"Oh," says one, "I can keep teetotal without signing your Pledge."

"Yes," says another, "it is childish to sign away
your freedom."

"It may be all very well," says a third, "for some to do it, but it is not so for me."

Why, then, should we sign the Pledge of Total Abstinence?

Sign the pledge: it is your protest against strong drink.—It is time for every thoughtful person to enter a solemn protest against strong drink, which every year is inflicting such awful havoc. Who can be indifferent to the woes it brings on hearts and homes, on villages and towns, on countries and continents? Well may the Hindoos call it "Shame-water." There is hardly a house in which you may not find its slain. There is not a newspaper that does not record its diabolical outrages. There is not a public officer that could not bear damning evidence against it.

We can not do much, but let us do what we can. We have a voice, a right to cry aye or nay, a power to assent or protest. Let us use them by all means on the right side. And if we cannot express our feeling in any other way, let us at least sign a solemn declaration on paper that we will never again touch the cruelest foe that ever reveled in human tears and blood.

Sign the pledge: it will benefit your health.—Alcohol is not more necessary to health than any other chemical or medicinal agent. It excites the heart, hinders digestion, disturbs the liver, and stupefies the brain. It gives a momentary glow and stimulus, but you have to pay for them afterward by an inevitable lessening of vital heat and animal power and mental force. Even in moderate quantities it acts as an irritant and a poison.

The athlete, in training for a boat-race, a prize-fight or a running match, must forego the use of alcohol; and if men do not want it for such extraordinary exertions, why do you want it for ordinary ones? English expeditions in Abyssinia, the Transvaal and Egypt, proved that if a General wished his troops to perform forced marches, or to undergo unusual fatigues, he must substitute coffee for grog. The extremes of the Arctic circle and the tropical sun are best endured on cold water, as the experience of many explorers and travelers proves. The tables of insurance offices show that one hundred moderate drinkers die for every seventy-three abstainers, and many offices have a special section to give abstainers the benefits of insurance at a lower price.

It would be a perfect revelation to some who read these words if they would give total abstinence a trial. Your appetites would be better, your minds would be clearer, your nerves would be stronger, and your whole system would get fitness and tone.

Sign the pledge: it will save your time.—We have only one short life to live, and we can not afford to fling the diamond moments into the rushing stream beside us. How many days in the fore part of the week are spent by our working-classes in taverns which are a dead loss to them and their families and the country! How many hours are spent by clerks and commercial travelers in the course of the week, at the bars of railway stations and restaurants, which might be sown with the seeds of golden harvest! How many evenings are worse than wasted in convivial company, which might be spent in innocent and health-giving recreation, or in acquiring knowledge which would unlock many a shut door! From all this you would escape, if you signed the Pledge.

Sign the pledge: it will save your purse.—Sit down and calculate how much you spend a day in drink, not only for yourself, but also for those whom you treat. It will amount to a respectable sum in the course of the year. Add to this the money you might earn in the time you now lose. Add to this all the sums squandered wastefully in the company into which habits of drinking lead you. And when all is put together, would it not make a nice amount against a rainy day, or for illness and old age?

I often say to those who sign my pledge cards that there is a $500 note hidden inside the double cardboard.

Sign the pledge: it will save you from temptation.—You have no intention of becoming a drunkard; you scorn the thought. But there is a risk of your becoming one, so long as you tamper with the drink. You take it now for the sake of society, but you will come to take it for its own sake. You cannot be sure that daily dram-drinking may not do for you what it has done for myriads, in exciting a thirst, now perhaps dormant, but which, when once aroused, will be unsatiable. Wise men, good men, strong men have been mastered by that awful thirst, who no more expected such a thing than you do. Is it not folly, then, for *you* to run the risk of creating it? Why not stop at once, before that thirst has been aroused?

You tell me that it seems hard for you to do without the drink. Then *that* is a sure sign that the accursed appetite has got a foothold within you. Spring off the car ere it rushes down the incline. Run the boat into a creek ere it is caught by the rapids above the falls. Force the cloven foot back out of the door before the demon has time to thrust his whole body into your heart and life. Do it at once. Do it now. You ask not to be led into temptation, then don't go into it. Taverns are well-called "shades" and "vaults." They are the shades of death, and vaults for the burial of all that is noblest and best in men. Avoid them. Pass them by. Refuse to enter them unless the Good Shepherd sends you there to find a lost sheep.

Sign the pledge: it will make a definite starting point in your history.—In all efforts after a better life it is well to have some landmark or time mark to which to look back and from which to date. There is a sort of satisfaction in being able to point to a mental stone-heap, or crease-line, or white-painted post, standing out on the moorland of life, and to say:

"Up to that point I lived a selfish, evil life, but

since then I have tried to run fair and well, by the help of God."

With some it is a sermon. With others it is a birthday, a death, an entry in the diary, or a New Year's Eve. With others it is the visit of some Gospel temperance advocate to their town. But in many cases, the same purpose is served by signing the pledge. The date of that pledge-card is a birthday, a new start, a beginning of a new era in the story of the soul; and it very often leads to the second step of faith in Christ.

Sign the pledge: it makes a strong obligation.— When a man gives up the drink, he must do all that can be done to strengthen his resolution. If he simply makes a resolution, he feels at liberty to withdraw from it if he choose. But if he double-knots his resolution with a solemn promise to which he has put his hand, then he feels bound by the most solemn obligations. He dare not violate his plighted troth. And in the moment of temptation, his self-respect, his love for truth, his desire to be a man of his word, his written vow, will be a strong reason for saying No.

A gentleman who signed the pledge-card recently said that during the whole of the next day he carried it in his pocket, and took it out fifteen times to remind him that he had put his hand to a promise which he dared not violate, and could not retract.

Sign the pledge: it will give a sufficient answer to those who tempt you to drink.—There is no answer that a man can give so good as this. If he refuses because he is hot, he will be advised to drink to get cool. If he refuses because he is cold, he will be recommended to drink to get warm. If he refuses because he can not afford it, his companion will gladly treat him. If he refuses because he is not well, there is no ailment to which flesh is heir for which intoxicating drinks are not prescribed as a certain cure. Men who are well drink till they are ill; and then drink to get themselves well again. None of these excuses avail, but if a man says, "I have signed the pledge," they may think him a fool, but they cannot say that he has not given a sufficient reason; and if they are true men themselves, they dare not ask him to break his word. If a man asks you to drink after you have signed the pledge, he is no true friend; he is doing the devil's work. He is certain to turn round and insult you after you have done his will, because he will have lost the last fragment of respect for you.

There are some men who must have a reason to give others for doing as they do. Here at least is a clear, straightforward, intelligible reason, which puts an end to controversy, and settles the matter forever—"I have signed the pledge."

Sign the pledge: it keeps it from becoming the badge of a reclaimed drunkard.—If the pledge were only signed by men who had been drunkards, but who were trying to live a new life, it would become the badge of reclaimed drunkards, and it would soon cease to be signed by this class of men who need it most. This would be a great calamity.

"I dare not sign the pledge," said a young doctor to a friend who was trying to get him to do so, as a means of saving him from ruin.

"Why not?" was his friend's reply.

"Because, if people heard that I had done so, they would say that there must have been a screw loose in my character, and that I was a reclaimed drunkard."

"No," said his friend, "they never can say that, for it has been signed by thousands of thousands on whose character there has never been a stain."

The answer reassured him. He took the pledge, and is become an earnest Christian worker.

You may not need to sign the pledge for yourself, but sign it that you may give the benefit, the weight, the standing of your own moral character. If every one of reputable and stainless character were to stand aloof, the pledge would be a hopeless failure. Every respectable Christian person who signs it is like one of the corks floating on the surface of the sea, helping to sustain the heavy nets laden with fish.

Sign the pledge: it makes it easier for others to do the same.—We are creatures of fashion. We cannot help it. We are made so. What one does, the others are apt to do. There's many an eager eye looking to see what the reader of these lines is going to do. If he signs the pledge, that boy, that companion, that servant, will do the same; but if he refuses to do so, it may be that the waiting one will also refuse, and that refusal will lead to ruin.

More eyes are watching us than we think. More

lives than we know are on the balance, waiting for
the feather of our example to turn them this way or
that. Are we right in leaving anything undone that
might save one for whom Christ died? We must use
all means to save some, though the use of the means
compel us to forego some boasted liberty, or some
loved indulgence.

Don't say that you have no influence. It is only
an excuse, you have; you would not like another to
say that.

"I have no influence," said a man to one who
asked him to take the pledge for the sake of others.

His wife came up at that moment and said, "That's
true, you have no more influence than a cat."

"If you say that again, woman," said he, "I will
knock you down."

Of course you have influence. Use it well.

Sign the pledge: it will win you friends.—We all
need friends, and if we have given up those who
gather round the drink, we need others, and we are
most likely to find these wherever there are pledge-
cards to be had for signature. It is all very well to
resolve to give up drink and to keep the vow secretly;
but it is much better to take the pledge in the presence of one or more persons, who shall bear witness
to what they have seen, and who will be bound to
you in the bonds of a new and common brotherhood,
because they have done the same thing, and are
pledged to the same cause.

OBJECTIONS

But I do not like to sign away my liberty.—Then, if you are unmarried, you will never be married; you will surely never promise to love and honor any one individual, because you may want to change your mind. And what is true in this case is true in others, and is a sufficient answer to the objection.

If you like, take the pledge *for a short time only,* as you take the lease of a house. You can easily renew it again and again. Or, better still, promise to abstain, by God's help, from all intoxicating drinks, as a beverage, *until you return your pledge-card to a friend.* This will give *you* an opportunity of relinquishing it when you choose, and it will give *him* an opportunity of speaking earnestly with you when your purpose is faltering.

But I may be forced to drink.—If you are, you will not violate your pledge. You only promise to abstain from intoxicants *as a beverage.* If it is poured down your throat by force, or when you are fainting; if the physician compels you to take it; if you take it unawares in some dish of cookery; your pledge is not broken. It is not you that break it.

But I have taken it, and broken more than once.— Then take it again, in humble dependence on the Saviour, who has been manifested to destroy the works of the devil (1 John 3:8).

Most, if not all, total abstinence pledges lay stress on the words—GOD HELPING ME. These words are the heart of all. If they are not felt deep down in the soul, the pledge is not good for much, it rests on mere human strength. But when God is appealed to, the case is altered. Divine power pours into the spirit which is lifted up to Him in prayer and trust. Angel hands are stretched out to hold back the erring feet. A holy garrison is put inside the weak and trembling nature to hold it against the foe. Ask the Lord Jesus to forgive the past. Ask Him to save you from your enemy. Ask Him to shield you in the day of battle. Ask Him, when the door is nearly battered in, to put His foot against it and keep it closely shut. He is able to keep you from stumbling. He is able to keep that which you commit to Him. He is able to make you more than a conqueror. Put yourself into His hands before you leave your room in the morning. Keep looking to Him all day. Praise Him for His grace each night.

"What's that, that you keep mumbling to yourself?" said a working man to another at a little distance from him in the same shop.

"I keep on saying 'Lord help me,' " was the reply; "I say it day and night. It is the only way I know of to keep down my thirst for the drink."

Take heart, my friends. The battle may be sharp, but victory is sure. And when once you stand firm on the rock, be on the alert to rescue others from the raging waters of strong drink.

CHAPTER 6

Burdens, and What to Do with Them

DO YOU KEEP the Sabbath? Not indeed the literal seventh-day rest, but the inner rest of which that day was the blessed type. The pause in the outward business of life was but a parable of that inner hush, which is not for one day but for all days; not for one race but for all men; not for the hereafter only but for now. The Sabbath-keeping which awaits the people of God, undiminished in a single atom by the storms which have swept around it, is for all faithful souls, who may take it when they will and carry it with them.

> Through dusky lane and wrangling mart,
> Plying their daily task with busier feet,
> Because their secret souls a holy strain repeat.

A strain borrowed from the eternal chords and harmonies of the life and being of God.

The secret of sabbath-keeping is in the absence of burden-bearing. "Thus saith the Lord, Take heed to yourselves and bear no burden on the Sabbath day, nor bring it in by the gates of Jerusalem. Neither

75

carry forth a burden out of your houses on the Sabbath day." And in the words that follow, the continual presence of a king is made to hinge on obedience about burdens (Jer. 17:24, etc.). Nehemiah
was so urgent in this matter that he set his servants
at the city gates, as they crowned the gray summit of
Zion, "that there should be no burden brought in on
the Sabbath day" (Neh. 13:19).

And what was true in those bygone days is true always. There can be no true Sabbath-keeping when
burdens are freely brought into the precincts of the
soul. As well try to sleep when a party of high-
spirited, healthy children are tearing up and down
the house, and playing hide-and-seek in all the
rooms. Care will break the rest of the soul as much
as sin does. And there is no hope that we should
know the peace which passeth all understanding till
we have learned the art of shutting the door against
the long train of burden-carrying thoughts which are
always coming up the hill from the world beneath to
fill our spirit with the ring of their feet and the
clamor of their cries.

We need not stay to describe *the results which
burden-bearing brings to the heavy-laden.* They are
evident in the careworn look, the weary eye, the
heavy step. But deeper than these, there is no power
in prayer, no joy in God, no lying down in green
pastures, no walking beside the waters of rest. As
snowflakes in the arctics or sand-grains in the tropics
will build a rampart before some lowly dwelling suffi-

cient to exclude the light, so will worries, each infinitesimal in itself, shut out the blessed light of God
from the soul and make midnight where God meant
midday.

Burden-bearing sadly dishonors God. As men of
the world look upon the faces of those who profess
to be God's children, and see them dark with the
same shadows as are flung across their own, they
may well wonder what sort of a Father He is. Whatever be a man's professions, we can not helping judging him by the faces of his children. And if God be
judged by the unconscious report made of Him by
some of His children, the hardest things ever said
against Him by His foes are not far from the truth.

Under such circumstances the unbeliever may fitly
argue, "Either there is no God, or He is powerless to
help, or He does not really love, or He is careless
of the needs of His children. Of what good will re-
ligion be to me?"

We are either libels or Bibles; harbor-lights or
warning-signals; magnetic or repellent; and which
very much depends on how we treat our burdens.

Of course there is a *difference between Care and
Pain;* between bearing the self-made burden of our
anxieties, and suffering according to the will of God.
We must not make light of sufferings sent by our
Father to teach lessons which could only be learned
in the school in which our Lord and Saviour has sat
before us to learn obedience. The chastened spirit
must go softly, and withdraw itself to suffer. But

this is very different from burden-bearing. There will be no doubt as to the Father's care, no worry about the issues, no foreboding as to the long future, which to the eye of faith gleams like the horizon-rim of the sea on which the sun is shining in splendor, though dark clouds brood immediately overhead.

Before we are thoroughly awake in the morning we sometimes become conscious of a feeling of depression, as if all were not right; and a voice seems to tell a long tale of burdens to be carried, and difficulties to be met as the hours pass by.

"Ah!" says the voice, "a miserable day will *this* be."

"How so?" we inquire, fearfully.

"Remember there is that creditor to meet, that skein to disentangle, that irritation to soothe, those violent tempers to confront. It is no use praying. Better linger where you are, and then drag through the day as you can. You are like a martyr being led to his death."

And too often we have yielded to the suggestion, and have dragged ourselves wearily through the hours, doing our daily tasks with hands engaged and strength spent by the burdens which we have assumed. God is pledged to give strength for all duties which He sets, but not for the burdens which we elect to take on as well.

The one cure for burden-bearing is to cast all burdens on the Lord. The margin of the revised version of Psalm 55:22 reads thus: *Cast that He hath given thee upon the Lord.* Whatever burden the Lord hath given thee, give it back to Him. Treat the burden of care as once the burden of sin; kneel down and deliberately hand it over to Jesus. Say to Him, "Lord, I entrust to Thee this, and this, and this. I can not carry them, they are crushing me; but I definitely commit them all to Thee to manage, and adjust, and arrange. Thou hast taken my sins. Take my sorrows, and in exchange give me Thy Peace, Thy Rest." As George Herbert says so quaintly, "We must put them all into Christ's bag."

Will not our Lord Jesus be at least as true and faithful as the best earthly friend we have ever known? And have there not been times in all our lives when we have been too weary or helpless to help ourselves, and have thankfully handed some wearing anxiety to a good, strong man, sure that when once it was entrusted to him, he would not rest until he had finished it to his satisfaction? And surely He who loved us enough to die for us may be trusted to arrange all the smaller matters of our daily lives!

Of course there are one or two *conditions* which we must fulfill, before we shall be able to hand over our burdens to the Lord Jesus, and leave them with Him in perfect confidence. We must have cast our sins on Him before we can cast our cares. We must be at peace with God through the work of our Saviour before we can have the peace of God through faith in His gracious interposition on our behalf. We must also be living on God's plan, tarrying under the

cloud, obeying His laws and executing His plans so
far as we know them. We must also feed faith with
promise, for this food is essential to make it thrive.
And when we have done all this we shall not find it
so difficult

> To kneel, and cast our load,
> E'en while we pray upon our God,
> Then rise with lightened cheer.

HAND OVER TO CHRIST THE BURDEN OF HOW TO GROW IN GRACE

This is a very great burden to some earnest people.
They go from convention to convention, from one
speaker to another, notebook in hand, so eager to
get the blessing (as they term it), and often thinking
more of the rapture of the gift than of the Person of
the Giver. And because they hear of others having
experiences which they know not, they carry heavy
burdens of disappointment and self-reproach.

Equally well might a child in kindergarten fret
because he is not entered in the higher classes of the
school. But why should he worry about his future
progress? His one business is to acquire the lessons
set him by his teacher. When those are learned it
will be *for him* to teach his pupil more, and advance
him to positions where quicker progress may be
made. And it is for us to learn the lessons which the
Lord Jesus sets before us day by day, leaving Him to
lead us into the fuller knowledge and love of God.

Thomas was one of the dull pupils in our Master's school. He could not see what was clear to all beside. But instead of chiding him, and leaving him to grope in the dark, the Master paid him a special visit, and made the glad fact of His resurrection so simple that the doubter was able to rejoice with the rest. Don't worry about your dullness; it will only mean that the dear Master will give you longer and more personal attention. Mothers give most pains to the sickly, weak, and stupid among their children.

HAND OVER TO CHRIST THE BURDEN OF MAINTAINING A CHRISTIAN PROFESSION

Many are kept from identifying themselves openly with the Lord's people by a secret feeling that they will never be able to hold out. They carry with them a nervous dread of bringing disgrace on their Christian profession, and trailing Christ's colors in the dust. Almost unconsciously, they repeat the words of David, "I shall now perish one day by the hand of Saul" (1 Sam. 27:1).

Anxiety about so sacred a matter as this will hide the face of Christ, as the impalpable vapor-wreaths hide the majestic, snow-capped peaks. And it is quite needless. He who saved can uphold. As is His heart of love, so is His arm of might. He is able to keep from stumbling, and present us faultless before the presence of His glory. But we shall never know the sufficiency of that keeping while we cling to the boat, or even keep one hand upon its side. Only when we have stepped right out on the water, relying utterly on the Master's power, shall we know how blessedly and certainly He keeps what is committed to Him against that day.

We must not carry even the burden of daily abiding in Him. Let us rather trust Him to keep us trusting and abiding in Himself. He will not fail us if we do, and will answer our faith by giving us an appetite for those exercises of prayer, Bible study, and communion, which are the secrets of unbroken fellowship.

HAND OVER TO CHRIST THE BURDEN OF CHRISTIAN WORK

How to maintain our congregations; how to hold our ground amid the competition of neighboring workers; how to sustain the vigor and efficiency of our machinery; how to adjust the differences arising between fellow and subordinate workers; how to find material enough for sermons and addresses—beneath the pressure of burdens like these how many workers break down! They could bear the work, but not the worry.

And yet the responsibility of the work is not ours but our Master's. He is bearing this world in His arms, as a mother her sick child. He is ministering to the infinite need of man. He is carrying on His great redemptive scheme for the glory of His Father. All He wants of us is a faithful performance of the daily tasks He gives.

Let the sailor-lad sleep soundly in his hammock; the captain knows exactly the ship's course. Let the errand-boy be content to fetch and carry, as he is bidden; the heads of the firm know what they are about, and have plenty of resources to meet all their needs. And let the Christian worker guard against bearing burdens which the Lord alone can carry. The Lord would never have sent us to His work without first calculating His ability to carry us through.

Hand Over to Christ the Burden of the Ebb and Flow of Feeling

Our feelings are as changeable as April weather. They are affected by an infinite number of subtle causes—our physical health, the state of the atmosphere, over-weariness, want of sleep—as well as by those which are spiritual and inward. No stringed instrument is more liable to be affected by minute changes than we are. And we are apt to take it sorely to heart when we see the tide of emotion running out fast.

At such times we should question ourselves, to see whether our lack of feeling is due to conscious sin or worrying; and if not, we may hand over all further anxiety in the matter to Him who knows our frame, and remembers that we are dust. And as we pass down the dark staircase, let us hold fast to the handrail of His will, willing to do His will, though in the dark. "I am as much Thine own, equally devoted

to Thee now in the depths of my soul, as when I
felt happiest in Thy love."

HAND OVER TO CHRIST ALL OTHER BURDENS

Servants with their frequent changes; employers
with unreasonable demands; unkind gossip and slan-
derous tales which are being circulated about you;
the perplexities and adversities of business; the difficulties to make two ends meet; the question of chang-
ing your residence, or situation, and obtaining another; children with the ailments of childhood and
the waywardness of youth; provision for sickness and
old age. There are some whose businesses are pecul-
iarly trying, and liable to cause anxious thoughts;
others whose horizon is always bounded by the gaunt
specters of poverty.

Any one of these will break our rest, as one bark-
ing dog may break our slumber in the stillest night,
and as one grain of dust in the eye will render it in-
capable of enjoying the fairest prospect.

There is nothing for us, then, but roll our burden,
and indeed, ourselves, on God (Ps. 22:8, marg.).
When a little boy, trying to help his father move
some books, fell on the stairs beneath the weight of
a heavy volume, the father ran to his aid and caught
up boy and burden both, and bore them in his arms
to his own room. And will our Father do worse? He
must love us infinitely, and be ever at hand. "He
careth for you" (1 Pet. 5:7).

It is a good way in dealing with God, and if you

are not quite sure of His will, to say that you will stay where you are, or go on doing what you have been doing, until He makes quite clear what He wants and empowers you to do. Roll the responsibility of your way on God (Prov. 16:3, marg.), and expect that He will make known to you any alteration which He desires in a way so unmistakable, that though you are dull and stupid you may not mistake.

Don't worry about dress, or ornaments, or doubtful things. Satan loves to turn the soul's attention from Christ to itself. It is as if a girl should spend an hour in her room wondering in what dress to meet her lover, who is waiting impatiently below. Let her go to him, and if she desires it, he will soon enough tell her clearly what he prefers. Get into the presence of Jesus, and you will not be left to hazy questionings and doubtful disputations, but will be told clearly and unmistakably His will, and always definitely about one point at a time.

Archbishop Leighton sweetly says: "When thou art either to do or suffer anything, when thou art about any purpose of business, go, tell God about it, and acquaint Him with it—yea, burden Him with it—and thou hast done for matter of caring. No more care, but sweet, quiet diligence in thy duty, and dependence on Him for the carriage of thy matters. Roll over on God, make one bundle of all: roll thy cares, and thyself with them, as one burden, all on thy God."

And so, when no burdens are brought into the

soul, but are handed immediately over to the blessed Lord, the peace of God will fill the inner temple. And though outside there may be the strife of tongues, and the chafe of this restless world, like the troubled sea when it cannot rest, and the pressure of many engagements, yet these things shall expand themselves on the battlements of the life which is the environing presence of God; while, within, the soul keeps an unbroken Sabbath, like the unruffled ocean depths, which are not stirred by the hurricanes that churn the surface into foam and fury. "The peace of God, which passeth all understanding, shall garrison your hearts and minds through Christ Jesus" (Phil. 4:7).

CHAPTER 7

How to Bear Sorrow

YOU ARE PASSING THROUGH a time of deep sorrow. The love on which you were trusting has suddenly failed you, and dried up like a brook in the desert— now a dwindling stream, then shallow pools, and at last drought. You are always listening for footsteps that do not come, waiting for a word that is not spoken, pining for a reply that tarries overdue.

Perhaps the savings of your life have suddenly disappeared. Instead of helping others, you must be helped; or you must leave the warm nest where you have been sheltered from life's storms to go alone into an unfriendly world; or you are suddenly called to assume the burden of some other life, taking no rest for yourself till you have steered it through dark and difficult seas into the haven. Your health, or sight, or nervous energy is failing; you carry in yourself the sentence of death; and the anguish of anticipating the future is almost unbearable. In other cases there is the sense of recent loss through death, like the gap in the forest, where the woodsman has lately been felling trees.

At such times life seems almost unsupportable. Will every day be as long as this? Will the slow-moving hours ever again quicken their pace? Will life ever array itself in another garb than the torn autumn remnants of past summer glory? "Hath God forgotten to be gracious? Hath He in anger shut up His tender mercies?" (Ps. 77:9).

This road has been trodden by myriads.—When you think of the desolating wars which have swept through every country and devastated every land; of the expeditions of the Nimrods, the Nebuchadnezzars, the Timours, the Napoleons of history; of the merciless slave trade; and of all the tyranny, the oppression, the wrong which the weak and defenseless have suffered at the hands of their fellows; of the unutterable sorrows of women and children—surely you must see that by far the larger number of our race have passed through the same bitter griefs as those which rend your heart.

Jesus Christ Himself trod this difficult path, leaving traces of His blood on its flints; and apostles, prophets, confessors, and martyrs have passed by the same way. It is comforting to know that others have traversed the same dark valley, and that the great multitudes which stand before the Lamb, wearing palms of victory, came out of great tribulation. Where they were we are; and, by God's grace, where they are we shall be.

Do not talk about punishment.—You may talk of chastisement or correction, for our Father deals with

us as with sons; or you may speak of reaping the results of mistakes and sins dropped as seeds into life's
furrows in former years; or you may have to bear the
consequences of the sins and mistakes of others; but
do not speak of punishment. Surely all the guilt and
penalty of sin were laid on Jesus, and He put them
away forever. His were the stripes and the chastisement of our peace. If God punishes us for our sins,
it would seem that the sufferings of Christ were in-
complete; and if He once began to punish us, life
would be too short for the infliction of all that we
deserve. Besides, how could we explain the anoma-
lies of life, and the heavy sufferings of the saints as
compared with the gay life of the ungodly? Surely,
if our sufferings were penal, there would be a reversal
of these lots.

Sorrow is a refiner's crucible.—It may be caused
by the neglect or cruelty of another, by circumstances
over which the sufferer has no control, or as the direct result of some dark hour in the long past; but
inasmuch as God has permitted it to come, it must
be accepted as His appointment, and considered as
the furnace by which He is searching, testing, prob-
ing, and purifying the soul. Suffering searches us as
fire does metals. We think we are fully for God, until
we are exposed to the cleansing fire of pain. Then
we discover, as Job did, how much dross there is in
us, and how little real patience, resignation, and
faith. Nothing so detaches us from the things of this
world, the life of sense, the birdlime of earthly affec-

tions. There is probably no other way by which the power of the self-life can be arrested, that the life of Jesus may be manifested in our mortal flesh.

But God always keeps the discipline of sorrow in His own hands.—Our Lord said, "My Father is the husbandman." His hand holds the pruning-knife. His eye watches the crucible. His gentle touch is on the pulse while the operation is in progress. He will not allow even the devil to have his own way with us. As in the case of Job, so always. The moments are carefully allotted. The severity of the test is exactly determined by the reserves of grace and strength which are lying unrecognized within, but will be sought for and used beneath the severe pressure of pain. He holds the winds in His fist, and the waters in the hollow of His hand. He dares not risk the loss of that which has cost Him the blood of His Son. "God is faithful, who will not suffer you to be [*tried*] above that ye are able" (1 Cor. 10:13).

In sorrow the Comforter is near.—"Very present in time of trouble." He *sits* by the crucible, as a Refiner of silver, regulating the heat, marking every change, waiting patiently for the scum to float away, and His own face to be mirrored in clear, translucent metal. No earthly friend may tread the winepress with you, but the Saviour is there, His garments stained with the blood of the grapes of your sorrow. Dare to repeat it often, though you do not feel it, and though Satan insists that God has left you, *"Thou art with me."* Mention His name again and

again, *"Jesus,* JESUS, Thou art with me." So you
will become conscious that He is there.

When friends come to console you they talk of
time's healing touch, as though the best balm for
sorrow were to forget; or in their well-meant kind-
ness they suggest travel, diversion, amusement, and
show their inability to appreciate the black night
that hangs over your soul. So you turn from them
sick at heart, and prepared to say, as Job, "Miserable
comforters are ye all." But all the while Jesus is
nearer than they are, understanding how they wear
you, knowing each throb of pain, touched by fellow-
feeling, silent in a love too full to speak, waiting to
comfort from hour to hour as a mother her weary
and suffering babe.

Be sure to study the art of this Divine comfort,
that you may be able to comfort them that are in any
affliction with the comfort with which you yourself
have been comforted of God (2 Cor. 1:4). There
can be no doubt that some trials are permitted to
come to us, as to our Lord, for no other reason than
that by means of them we should become able to
give sympathy and succor to others. And we should
watch with all care each symptom of the pain, and
each prescription of the Great Physician, since in all
probability at some future time we shall be called
to minister to those passing through similar experiences. Thus we learn by the things which we suffer,
and, being made perfect, become authors of priceless and eternal help to souls in agony.

Do not shut yourself up with your sorrow.—A friend, in the first anguish of bereavement, wrote, saying that he must give up the Christian ministries in which he had delighted; and I replied immediately, urging him not to do so, because there is no solace for heart-pain like ministry. The temptation of great suffering is toward isolation, withdrawal from the life of men, sitting alone, and keeping silence. Do not yield to it. Break through the icy chains of reserve, if they have already gathered. Arise, anoint your head and wash your face; go forth to your duty, with willing though chastened steps.

Selfishness of every kind, in its activities or its introspection, is a hurtful thing, and shuts out the help and love of God. Sorrow is apt to be selfish. The soul, occupied with its own griefs, and refusing to be comforted, becomes presently a Dead Sea, full of brine and salt, over which the birds do not fly, and beside which no green thing grows. And thus we miss the very lesson that God would teach us. His constant war is against the self-life, and every pain He inflicts is to lessen its hold upon us. But we may thwart His purpose and extract poison from His gifts, as men get opium and alcohol from innocent plants.

A Hindoo woman, the beautiful Eastern legend tells us, lost her only child. Wild with grief, she implored a prophet to give back her little one to her love. He looked at her for a long while tenderly, and said:

"Go, my daughter, bring me a handful of rice from a house into which Death has never entered, and I will do as thou desirest."

The woman at once began her search. She went from dwelling to dwelling, and had no difficulty in obtaining the rice the prophet specified; but when they had granted it, she inquired:

"Are you all here around the hearth—father, mother, children—none missing?"

The people invariably shook their heads, with sighs and looks of sadness. Far and wide as she wandered, there was always some vacant seat by the hearth. And gradually, as she passed on, the legend says, the waves of her grief subsided before the spectacle of sorrow everywhere; and her heart ceased to be occupied with its own selfish pang, flowing out in strong yearnings of sympathy with the universal suffering. Tears of anguish softened into tears of pity, passion melted away in compassion, she forgot herself in the general interest, and found redemption in redeeming.

Do not chide yourself for feeling strongly.—Tears are natural. Jesus wept. A thunderstorm without rain is fraught with peril; the pattering raindrops cool the air and relieve the overcharged atmosphere. The swollen brooks indicate that the snows are melting on the hills and spring is near. "Daughters of Jerusalem," said our Lord, "weep for yourselves and your children."

To bear sorrow with dry eyes and stolid heart may

befit a Stoic, but not a Christian. We have no need to rebuke fond nature crying for its mate, its lost joy, the touch of the vanished hand, the sound of the voice that is still, provided only that the will is resigned. This is the one consideration for those who suffer—*Is the will right?* If it isn't, God Himself cannot comfort. If it is, then the path will inevitably lead from the valley of the shadow of death to the banqueting table and the overflowing cup.

Many say: "I can not feel resigned. It is bad enough to have my grief to bear, but I have this added trouble, that I can not *feel* resigned."

My invariable reply is: "You probably never can feel resignation, but you can *will* it."

The Lord Jesus, in the Garden of Gethsemane, has shown us how to suffer. He chose His Father's will. Though Judas, prompted by Satan, was the instrument for mixing the cup and placing it to the Saviour's lips, He looked right beyond him to the Father, who permitted him to work his cruel way, and said: "The cup that My Father giveth Me to drink, shall I not drink it?" And He said repeatedly, "If this cup may not pass from Me, except I drink it, Thy will be done." He gave up His own way and will, saying, "I will Thy will, O My Father. Thy will, and not Mine, be done."

Let all sufferers who read these lines go apart and dare to say the same words: "Thy will, and not mine. Thy will be done in the earth of my life, as in the heaven of Thy purpose. I choose Thy will." Say this thoughtfully and deliberately, not because you can *feel* it, but because you *will* it; not because the way of the cross is pleasant, but because it must be right. Say it repeatedly, whenever the surge of pain sweeps through you, whenever the wound begins to bleed afresh. "Not my will, but Thine be done." *Dare to say Yes to God.* "Even so, Father, for so it seemeth good in Thy sight."

And so you will be led to feel that all is right and well. A great calm will settle down on your heart, a peace that passeth understanding, a sense of rest, which is not inconsistent with suffering, but walks in the midst of it as the three young men in the fiery furnace, to whom the burning coals must have been like the dewy grass of a forest glade.

"The doctor told us my little child was dying. I felt like a stone. But *in a moment* I seemed to give up my hold on her. She appeared no longer mine, but God's."

Be sure to learn God's lessons.—Each sorrow carries at its heart a germ of holy truth, which if you get and sow in the soil of your heart will bear harvests of fruit, as seed-corns from mummy-cases bear fruit in modern soil. God has a meaning in each blow of His chisel, each incision of His knife. He knows the way that He takes. But His object is not always clear to us.

In suffering and sorrow God touches the minor chords, develops the passive virtues, and opens to view the treasures of darkness, the constellations of promise, the rainbow of hope, the silver light of the covenant. What is character without sympathy, submission, patience, trust, and hope that grips the unseen as an anchor? But these graces are only possible through sorrow. Sorrow is a garden, the trees of which are laden with the peaceable fruits of righteousness; do not leave it without bringing them with you. Sorrow is a mine, the walls of which glisten with precious stones; be sure and do not retrace your steps into daylight without some specimens. Sorrow is a school. You are sent to sit on its hard benches and learn from its black-lettered pages lessons which will make you wise forever; do not trifle away your chance of graduating there. Miss Havergal used to talk of "turned lessons"!

Count on the afterward.—God will not always be causing grief. He traverses the dull brown acres with His plough, seaming the yielding earth that He may be able to cast in the precious grain. Believe that in days of sorrow He is sowing light for the righteous, and gladness for the upright in heart. Look forward to the reaping. Anticipate the joy which is set before you, and which shall flood your heart with minstrel notes when patience has had her perfect work.

You will live to recognize the wisdom of God's choice for you. You will one day see that the thing you wanted was only second best. You will be surprised to remember that you once nearly broke your heart and spilled the wine of your life for what would never have satisfied you if you had caught it, as the

child the butterfly or soap-bubble. You will meet
again your beloved. You will have again your love.
You will become possessed of a depth of character,
a breadth of sympathy, a fund of patience, an ability
to understand and help others, which, as you lay
them at Christ's feet for Him to use, will make you
glad that you were afflicted. You will see God's plan
and purpose; you will reap His harvest; you will behold His face, and be satisfied. Each wound will
have its pearl; each carcass will contain a swarm of
bees; each foe, like Midian to Gideon, will yield its
goodly spoil.

The way of the cross, rightly borne, is the only
way to the everlasting light. The path that threads
the Garden of Gethsemane, and climbs over the hill
of Calvary, alone conducts to the visions of the
Easter morning and the glories of the Ascension
mount. If we will not drink of His cup, or be bap-
tized with His baptism, or fill up that which is behind of His sufferings, we cannot expect to share in
the joys of His espousals and the ecstasy of His
triumph. But if these conditions are fulfilled, we
shall not miss one note in the everlasting song, one
element in the bliss that is possible to men.

*Remember that somehow suffering rightly borne
enriches and helps mankind.*—The death of Hallam
was the birthday of Tennyson's *"In Memoriam."* The
cloud of insanity that brooded over Cowper gave us
the hymn, *"God moves in a mysterious way."* Mil-
ton's blunders taught him to sing of *"Holy light,*

offspring of heaven's first-born." Rist used to say, "The cross has pressed many songs out of me." And it is probable that none rightly suffer anywhere without contributing something to the alleviation of human grief, to the triumph of good over evil, of love over hate, and of light over darkness.

If you believe this, could you not bear to suffer? Is not the chief misery of all suffering its loneliness, and perhaps its apparent aimlessness? Then dare to believe that no man dieth to himself. Fall into the ground, bravely and cheerfully, to die. If you refuse this, you will abide alone; but if you yield to it, you will bear fruit which will sweeten the lot and strengthen the life of others who perhaps will never know your name, or stop to thank you for your help.

CHAPTER 8

In the Secret of His Presence

IN ONE SENSE God is always near us. He is not an Absentee, needing to be brought down from the heavens or up from the deep. He is nigh at hand. His Being pervades all being. Every world, that floats like an islet in the ocean of space, is filled with signs of His presence, just as the home of your friend is littered with the many evidences of his residence, by which you know that he lives there, though you have not seen his face. Every crocus pushing through the dark mold; every firefly in the forest; every bird that springs up from its nest before your feet; everything that is—*all* are as full of God's presence as the bush which burned with His fire, before which Moses bared his feet in acknowledgment that God was there.

But we do not always realize it. We often pass hours, and days, and weeks. We sometimes engage in seasons of prayer, we go to and fro from His house, where the ladder of communication rests; and still He is a shadow, a name, a tradition, a dream of days gone by.

"Oh! that I knew where I might find Him! that I might come even to His seat! . . . Behold, I go forward, but he is not there; and backward, but I cannot perceive him: on the left hand, where he doth work, but I cannot behold him: he hideth himself on the right hand, that I cannot see him" (Job 23:3, 8, 9).

How different is this failure to realize the presence of God to the blessed experience of His nearness realized by some.

Brother Lawrence, the simple-minded cook, for more than sixty years never lost the sense of the presence of God, but was as conscious of it while performing the duties of his humble office, as when partaking of the Holy Supper.

John Howe, on the blank page of his Bible, made this record in Latin: "This very morning I awoke out of a most ravishing and delightful dream, when a wonderful and copious stream of celestial rays, from the lofty throne of the Divine Majesty, seemed to dart into my open and expanded breast. I have often since reflected on that very signal pledge of special Divine favor, and have with repeated fresh pleasure tasted the delights thereof."

Are not these experiences, so blessed and inspiring, similar to that of the author of the longest, and in some respects, the sublimest Psalm in the Psalter? He had been beating out the golden ore of thought through the successive paragraphs of marvelous power and beauty, when suddenly he seems to have become conscious that He, of whom he had been

speaking, had drawn near, and was bending over
him. The sense of the presence of God was borne in
upon his inner consciousness. And, lifting up a face
on which reverence and ecstasy met and mingled, he
cried, *"Thou art near, O Lord!"* (Psalm 119:151.)

If only such an experience of the nearness of God
were always ours, infolding us as air or light; if only
we could feel, as the great Apostle put it on Mars'
Hill, that God is not far away, but the element in
which we have our being, as sea-flowers in deep, still
lagoons:—then we should understand what David
meant when he spoke about dwelling in the house
of the Lord all the days of his life, beholding His
beauty, inquiring in His temple, and hidden in the
secret of His pavilion (Ps. 27). Then, too, we should
acquire the blessed secret of *peace, purity* and *power.*

In the Secret of His Presence there is Peace. "In
the world ye shall have tribulation," our Master said,
"but in Me ye shall have peace." It is said that a
certain insect has the power of surrounding itself
with a film of air, encompassed in which it drops
into the midst of muddy, stagnant pools, and remains
unhurt. And the believer is also conscious that he
is enclosed in the invisible film of the Divine Presence, as a far-traveled letter in the envelope which
protects it from hurt and soil.

"They draw near me that follow after mischief,"
but Thou art nearer than the nearest, and I dwell in
the inner ring of Thy presence. The mountains round
about me are filled with the horses and chariots of

Thy protection. No weapon that is formed against me can prosper, for it can only reach me through Thee, and, touching Thee, will glance harmlessly aside. To be in God is to be in a well-fitted house when the storm has slipped from its leash; or in a sanctuary, the doors of which shut out the pursuer.

In the Secret of His Presence there is Purity. The mere vision of snow-capped Alps, seen from afar across Lake Geneva so elevates and transfigures the rapt and wistful soul as to destroy all evil things which would thrust themselves upon the inner life. The presence of a little child, with its guileless purity, has been known to disarm passion, as a beam of light, falling in a reptile-haunted cave, scatters the slimy snakes. But what shall not Thy presence do for me, if I acquire a perpetual sense of it, and live in its secret place? Surely, in the heart of that fire, black cinder though I be, I shall be kept pure, and glowing, and intense!

In the Secret of His Presence there is Power. My cry, day and night, is for power—spiritual power. Not the power of intellect, oratory, or human might. These cannot avail to vanquish the serried ranks of evil. Thou sayest truly that it is not by might nor power. Yet human souls which touch Thee become magnetized, charged with a spiritual force which the world can neither gainsay nor resist. Oh! let me touch Thee! Let me dwell in unbroken contact with Thee, that out of Thee successive tides of Divine energy may pass into and through my emptied and eager spirit, flowing, but never ebbing, and lifting me into a life of blessed ministry, which shall make deserts below like the garden of the Lord.

But how shall we get and keep this sense of God's nearness?

Must we go back to Bethel, with its pillar of stone, where even Jacob said, "Surely God is in this place"? Ah, we might have stood beside him, with un-anointed eye, and seen no ladder, heard no voice; while the patriarch would discover God in the bare moorlands of our lives, trodden by us without reverence or joy.

Must we travel to the mouth of the cave in whose shadow Elijah stood, thrilled by the music of the still small voice, sweeter by contrast with the thunder and the storm? Alas! we might have stood beside him unconscious of that glorious Presence; while Elijah, if living now, would discern it in the whisper of the wind, the babbling of babes, the rhythm of heart throbs.

If we had stationed ourselves in our present state beside the Apostle Paul when he was caught into the third Heaven, we should probably have seen nothing but a tent-maker's shop, or a dingy room in a hired lodging—we in the dark, while he was in transports; while he would discern, were he to live again, angels on our steamships, visions in our temples, doors opening into Heaven amid the tempered glories of our more somber skies.

In point of fact, we carry everywhere our circumference of light or dark. God is as much in the world as He was when Enoch walked with Him, and Moses communed with Him face to face. He is as willing to be a living, bright, glorious Reality to us as to them. But the fault is with us. Our eyes are unanointed because our hearts are not right. The pure in heart still see God, and to those who love Him, and do His commandments, He still manifests Himself as He does not to the world. Let us cease to blame our times; let us blame ourselves. We are degenerate, not they.

What, then, is that temper of soul which most readily perceives the presence and nearness of God? Let us endeavor to learn the blessed secret of abiding ever in the secret of His Presence and of being hidden in His pavilion (Ps. 31:20).

Remember, then, at the outset, that neither you nor any of our race, can have that glad consciousness of the Presence of God except *through Jesus.* None knoweth the Father but the Son and those to whom the Son reveals Him; and none cometh to the Father but by Him. Apart from Jesus the Presence of God is an object of terror, from which devils wish to hide themselves, and sinners weave aprons, or hide among the trees. But in Him all barriers are broken down, all veils rent, all clouds dispersed, and the weakest believer may live, where Moses sojourned, in the midst of the fire, before whose consuming flames no impurity can stand.

"What part of the Lord's work is most closely connected with this blessed sense of the Presence of God?"

It is through the blood of His cross that sinners are made nigh. In His death He not only revealed the tender love of God, but put away our sins, and wove for us those garments of stainless beauty, in which we are gladly welcomed into the inner presence-chamber of the King. Remember it is said, "I will commune with thee from off the mercy-seat." That golden slab on which Aaron sprinkled blood whenever he entered the most Holy Place was a type of Jesus. He is the true mercy-seat. And it is when you enter into deepest fellowship with Him in His death, and live most constantly in the spirit of His memorial supper, that you shall realize most deeply His nearness. Now, as at Emmaus, He loves to make Himself known in the breaking of bread.

"And is this all? for I have heard this many times, and still fail to live in the secret place as I would."

Exactly so; and therefore, to do for us what no effort of ours could do, our Lord has received of His Father the promise of the Holy Ghost, that He should bring into our hearts the very Presence of God. Understand that since you are Christ's, the blessed Comforter is yours. He is within you as He was within your Lord, and in proportion as you live in the Spirit, and walk in the Spirit, and open your entire nature to Him, you will find yourself becoming His Presence-chamber, irradiated with the light of His glory. And as you realize that He is in you, you will realize that you are ever in Him. Thus the beloved Apostle wrote, "Hereby know we that we dwell in Him, and He in us, because He hath given us of His Spirit" (1 John 4:13).

"All this I know, and yet I fail to realize this marvelous fact of the indwelling of the Spirit in me; how then can I ever realize my indwelling in Him?"

It is because your life is so hurried. You do not take time enough for meditation and prayer. The Spirit of God within you and the Presence of God without you cannot be discerned while the senses are occupied with pleasure, or the pulse beats quickly, or the brain is filled with the tread of many hurrying thoughts. It is when water stands that it becomes pellucid, and reveals the pebbly beach below. Be still, and know that God is within thee and around! In the hush of the soul the unseen becomes visible, and the eternal real. The eye dazzled by the sun cannot detect the beauties of its pavilion till it has had time to rid itself of the glare. Let no day pass without its season of silent waiting before God.

"Are there any other conditions which I should fulfill, so that I may abide in the secret of His Presence?"

Be pure in heart. Every permitted sin encrusts the windows of the soul with thicker layers of grime, obscuring the vision of God. But every victory over impurity and selfishness clears the spiritual vision, and there fall from the eyes, as it had been, scales. In the power of the Holy Ghost deny self, give no quarter to sin, resist the devil, and thou shalt see God.

The unholy soul could not see God even though it were set down in the midst of Heaven. But holy souls see God amid the ordinary commonplaces of earth, and find everywhere an open vision. Such could not be nearer God though they stood by the sea of glass. Their only advantage there would be that the veil of their mortal and sinful natures having been rent, the vision would be more direct and perfect.

Keep His commandments. Let there be not one jot or tittle unrecognized and unkept. *He that hath My commandments and keepeth them, he it is that loveth Me, and he that loveth Me shall be loved of My father, and I will love him, and will manifest Myself to him.* Moses the faithful servant was also the seer, and spake with God face to face as a man speaketh with his friend.

Continue in the spirit of prayer. Sometimes the vision will tarry to test the earnestness and steadfastness of thy desire. At other times it will come as the dawn steals over the sky, and, or ever you are aware, you will find yourself conscious that He is near. He was even accustomed to glide, unheralded, into the midst of His disciples through unopened doors. "Thy footsteps are not known" (Ps. 77:19).

At such times we may truly say with St. Bernard: "He entered not by the eyes, for His presence was not marked by color; nor by the ears, for there was no sound; nor by the breath, for He mingled not with the air; nor by the touch, for He was impalpable. You ask, then, how I knew that He was present. Because He was a quickening power. As soon as He entered, He awoke my slumbering soul. He moved and pierced my heart, which before was strange, stony, hard and sick, so that my soul could bless the Lord, and all that is within me praised His Holy Name."

Cultivate the habit of speaking aloud to God. Not perhaps always, because our desires are often too sacred or deep to be put into words. But it is well to acquire the habit of speaking to God as to a present friend while sitting in the house or walking by the way. Seek the habit of talking things over with God—thy letters, thy plans, thy hopes, thy mistakes, thy sorrows and sins. Things look very differently when brought into the calm light of His presence. One cannot talk long with God aloud without feeling that He is near.

Meditate much upon the Word. This is the garden where the Lord God walks, the temple where He dwells, the presence-chamber where He holds court, and is found by those who seek Him. It is through the word that we feed upon the Word. And He said, "He that eateth my flesh, and drinketh my blood, dwelleth in me and I in him" (John 6:56).

Be diligent in Christian work. The place of prayer is indeed the place of His manifested presence, but that presence would fade from it were we to linger there after the bell of duty had rung for us below. We shall ever meet it as we go about our necessary work: "Thou meetest him that worketh righteousness." As we go forth to our daily tasks the angel of His presence comes to greet us, and turns to go at our side. "Go ye," said the Master; "Lo, I am with you all the days." Not only in temple courts, or in sequestered glens, or in sick rooms, but in the round of daily duty, in the common-places of life, on the dead levels of existence, we may be ever in the secret of His presence, and shall be able to say with Elijah before Ahab, and Gabriel to Zacharias, "I stand in the presence of God" (1 Kings 17:1; Luke 1:19).

Cultivate the habit of recognizing the Presence of God. "Blessed is the man whom Thou choosest, and causest to approach unto Thee, that he may dwell in Thy courts." There is no life like this. To feel that God is with us; that He never leads us through a place too narrow for Him to pass as well; that we can never be lonely again, never for a single moment; that we are beset by Him behind and before, and covered by His hand; that He could not be nearer to us, even if we were in Heaven itself. To have Him as Friend, and Referee, and Counselor, and Guide. To realize that there is never to be a Jericho in our lives without the presence of the Captain of the Lord's host, with those invisible but mighty legions, before whose charge all walls must fall down. What wonder that the saints of old waxed valiant in fight as they heard Him say, "I will be with thee; I will not fail thee nor forsake thee" (Josh. 1:5).

Begone fear and sorrow and dread of the dark valley! "Thou shalt hide [me] in the secret of Thy presence from the pride of man; Thou shalt keep [me] secretly in a pavilion from the strife of tongues" (Ps. 31:20).

Chapter 9

The Fullness of the Spirit

"Be Filled with the Spirit."—Ephesians 5:18

NOTHING CAN COMPENSATE the Church, or the individual Christian, for the lack of the Holy Spirit. What the full stream is to the mill wheel, that the Holy Spirit is to the Church. What the principle of life is to the body, that the Holy Spirit is to the individual. We shall stand powerless and abashed in the presence of our difficulties and our foes until we learn what He can be, as a mighty tide of love and power in the hearts of His saints.

Among the readers of these lines there may be many who are suffering from different forms of spiritual weakness, all of which are directly attributable to the lack of the Holy Spirit. Not that they are completely destitute of Him, for if they were, they would not be Christians at all; but that, being within them, He is present only as an attenuated thread, a silver streak, a shallow brook. Why should we be content with this? The Pentecostal fullness, the enduement of power, the baptism of fire, are all within our reach. Let us be inspired with a holy ambition to get all that our God is willing to bestow.

It is not difficult to show this contrast by analogies drawn from the Word of God. May we not reverently say that the ministry of our blessed Lord Himself owed much of its marvelous power to that moment when, although filled with the Holy Spirit from His birth, He was afresh anointed at the waters of baptism? With marked emphasis it was said He was filled with the Spirit (Luke 4:1), and returned in the power of the Spirit unto Galilee (v. 14), and stood up in the synagogue of His native town, claiming the ancient prophecy, and declaring that the Spirit of God was upon Him (v. 18). His wondrous words and works are directly traced to the marvelous operation of the Holy Ghost upon His human life (Acts 10:38).

Do you lack *assurance?* Sometimes you do not, for you feel happy and content. But these happy hours are fled, and your rest is broken, as the surface of the mountain tarn is overcast and ruffled by the gathering storm. You need a basis of settled peace, and it is only to be found first, in a clear apprehension of what Jesus has done for you; secondly, in the sealing of the Holy Spirit. It is His sacred office to witness with our spirit that we are the children of God. He is the Spirit of adoption, whereby we cry, "Abba, Father!"

Do you lack *victory over sin?* This is not to be wondered at, if you neglect the Holy Spirit. He is the blessed antidote to the risings and dominion of the flesh. He lusts against the flesh, so that we may not fulfill its lusts. When He fills the heart in His glorious fullness, the suggestions of temptation are instantly quenched, as sparks in the ocean wave. Sin can no more stand against the presence of the Holy Spirit than darkness can resist the gentle, all-pervasive beams of morning light.

If, however, He is grieved, or resisted, or quenched, so that His power and presence are restrained, there is no deliverance for the spirit—however bitter its remorse, or eager its resort to fastings, mortification and regrets. The law of the Spirit of Life which is in Christ Jesus can alone make us free from the law of sin and death. But it can, and it will—if we only yield ourselves to its operation.

Do you lack the *fruits of holiness?* Some whom we know are so evidently filled with the fruits of righteousness, which are the praise of God, that we are instinctively drawn to them. Their faces are bright with the presence of the Lord, though they drink of the cup of His sorrows. Their spirit is tender; their disposition sweet and unselfish, and their childlike humility flings the halo of indescribable beauty over their whole behavior. We lack these graces. There is little in us to attract men to Christ; much to repel. Our boughs are naked and bare, as if locusts had stripped them. And the reason is evident. We have not let the Holy Spirit have His way with our inner life. Had the sap of His presence been mightily within us, we should have been laden with luscious fruitage; it would have been impossible to be otherwise.

Do you lack *power for service?* You have no burning thirst for the salvation of others. You are not on fire for souls. You have never been in agony over the alienation of men from God. And when you speak, there is no power in what you say. The devils laugh at your attempts to exorcise them. The sleeper turns for a moment uneasily, but soon falls into profounder slumber than ever. The home, the class, the congregation, yield no results. No hand-picked fruit fills your basket. No shoal of fish breaks your nets. No recruits accept your call to arms. And you cannot expect it to be otherwise till you obtain the power which our Lord promised when He said: "Ye shall receive the power of the Holy Ghost coming upon you." It was when the early Christians were filled with the Holy Ghost that they spake the word of God with boldness and gave witness with great power to the resurrection of the Lord Jesus.

These and many other deficiencies would be met, if only we were filled with the Holy Spirit. There would be a joy, a power, a consciousness of the Lord Jesus, an habitual rest in the will of God, which would be a joyful discovery to us; if only we refused to be satisfied with anything less than the full in-dwelling of the Holy Spirit.

Mr. Spurgeon said once that he never passed a single quarter of an hour in his waking moments

without a distinct consciousness of the presence of
the Lord. When the Spirit fills the heart, Jesus is
vividly real and evidently near. What is He to you?
Do you awake in the morning beneath His light
touch and spend the hours with Him? Can you fre-
quently look up from your work and perceive His
face? Are you constantly seeking from Him power,
grace, direction? If He is but a fitful vision, you
have not realized the first mark of the Pentecostal
gift.

Entire consecration to the service of the Lord
Jesus is a great step in advance of the experience of
most Christians; but even that is not enough. It is
often largely *negative;* but we require something
strongly *positive,* to meet the necessities of our hearts
and of our times. And this is to be sought in our entire possession by that mighty Spirit whose advent at
Pentecost has dated a new era for the Church and
the world.

Of course He was always in the world. It was the
Holy Spirit of Pentecost who brooded over chaos,
and spoke in prophets and holy men, and nerved the
heroes and saints of the Old Testament time. The
day of Pentecost did not introduce a new Spirit into
the world, but it inaugurated an era in which the
weakest and meanest of the saints might possess Him
in the same measure as they did who lived upon its
farther side. Before that momentous day His fullness was the prerogative of only the few, the *elite,*
the Elijahs, and Isaiahs and Daniels, but since that

day He has been shed forth in all His *plenitude on the many*—on women and children; on obscure thinkers and hidden workers; on hand-maids and servants; on all and any who were prepared to fulfill the conditions and to abide by the results. Why not on us?

We are willing to admit that the special gifts of the Holy Ghost belong to the Apostolic age. Given for a specific purpose, they are now withdrawn; though it is a serious question whether they might not have been continued, if only the Church had been more faithful to her sacred trust. But the special gifts of the Holy Ghost are altogether apart from His blessed fullness. That is not the exclusive right of any age. Confined to no limited era or epoch in the history of the Church, it pours its tide of light and power around us, as the Nile in flood; nor is there a single plot or garden-ground, however remote, into which it will not come, to fertilize and enrich, if only the channel of communication be kept cleansed and open.

Alas, that many think that the Almighty, like some bankrupt builder, constructed the portico of His Church with marble, and has finished it with common brick!

"Be filled with the Spirit" is an injunction as wide-reaching in its demands as "Husbands, love your wives," which is found on the same page. It is a positive command, which we must obey for our good, and all God's commands are enablings. In other

words, He is prepared to make us what He tells us to become. Moreover, on the day of Pentecost, in words which are the charter of our right to the fullness of the Holy Spirit, the Apostle Peter told the listening crowds that the fullness which had suddenly come on them from the ascended Lord—and which was a direct fulfillment of the ancient prophecy—was not for them only, or for their children; but for as many as were afar off, even for them whom the Lord God shall call. Are you one of His called ones? Then rejoice because that fullness is for you! Be not faithless, *but believing!* Lay claim at once to the covenanted portion, and thank God for having cast your lot in an age of such marvelous possibilities.

EXCITE HOLY DESIRE BY CONSIDERING WHAT THE FULLNESS OF THE SPIRIT MEANS

We cannot expect to have it if we are quite content to live without it. Our Father is not likely to entrust this priceless gift to those who are indifferent to its possession. Where the flame of desire burns low there can be no intelligent expectation that the Holy Spirit's fullness shall be realized.

And it is not enough to have a fitful and inconstant desire, which flames up today, but will remain dormant for months and years. There must be a steady purpose, able to stand the test of waiting (if need be) for ten days, and to bear the rebuff of silence or apparent denial.

And yet the flame of desire needs fuel. We must

muse before that fire can burn. And it becomes us, therefore, to stir up the gift that is within us by a quiet consideration of all that is meant by becoming Spirit-filled.

There is no book which will so move us in this direction as the Acts of the Apostles. It is perfectly marvelous to see what this fullness did for those who first received it. Cowards became brave. Obtuse intellects which had stumbled at the simplest truths, suddenly awoke to apprehend the Master's scheme. Bosoms that had heaved with rivalry and suspicion and desire for earthly power, now thought each better than himself and sought to excel in humble ministry to the saints. Such power attended their words that crowds became congregations, Christ's murderers became His worshipers and friends. Councils of clever men were not able to withstand the simple eloquence of indisputable facts. Towns and countries were shaken, and yielded converts by the thousand to the unlearned but fervid preachers of the cross.

All this was simply attributable to the power which had become the common property of the whole Church. *And there is not a fragment of reason why it should not do so much for us.* And, as we contrast that triumphant success to our halting progress, shall not we be filled with uncontrollable longings that He should work similar results by us?

We may still further secure the same results by

studying the biography of saintly men belonging to recent centuries. Happy the man within reach of a library, the shelves of which are well lined with books of holy biography! He will never, never be in want of additional stimulus as he reads the stories of McCheyne and W. C. Burns, of Brainerd and Martyn, of Jonathan Edwards and others. He will not envy or repine; but he will constantly lift eye and heart to Heaven, asking that as much may be done through himself.

And moreover the promises of the Scriptures are enough to incite us to the uttermost. That rivers of water should flow from us; that we should never need to be anxious about our words, because they would be given; that we should be taught all things, and led into the whole circle of truth; that we should know Christ, and be changed into His image; that we should have power—all this is so fascinating that it is impossible not to glow with a holy desire to be charged with the Holy Ghost, as a jar with electricity. And, if needs be, we shall be prepared to bear the test of long waiting, as the faithful few did in the upper room.

SEEK THIS BLESSED FULLNESS FROM THE RIGHT MOTIVE

If you want it that you may realize a certain experience, or attract people to yourself, or transform some difficulty into a stepping-stone, you are likely

to miss it. You must be set on the one purpose of
magnifying the Lord Jesus in your body, whether by
life or death. Ask that all inferior motives may be
destroyed, and that this may burn strong and clear
within you.

God will not find water for us to use for turning
our own water-wheels. He will do nothing to minister to our pride. He will not give us the Holy Spirit
to enable us to gain celebrity, or to procure a name,
or to live an easy, self-contented life.

If we seek the Holy Spirit merely for our happi-
ness, or comfort, or liberty of soul, it will be exceed-
ingly unlikely that He will be given. His one passion
is *the glory of the Lord Jesus;* and He can only make
His abode with those who are willing to be at one
with Him in this. "Can two walk together except
they be agreed?" But if you are actuated simply by
the desire that the Lord Jesus may be magnified in
you, whether by life or death; if you long, above all,
that men should turn away from you to Him, as they
did from John the Baptist—then rejoice, because
you are near blessing beyond words to describe. If
your motives fall below this standard, trust in Him
to enlighten and purify them, and offer Him a free
entrance within. It will not then be long ere there
shall be a gracious response; and the Lord, whom
you seek, shall suddenly come to His temple, and He
shall sit as a refiner of silver, that the sons of Levi
may offer an offering in righteousness (Mal. 3:1-3).

CONSIDER THAT HOLY SCRIPTURE IS
HIS SPECIAL ORGAN

A subtle danger besets the teaching of this most helpful doctrine, and one that we need to guard against. Some earnest people have magnified the inner light and leading of the Holy Spirit to the neglect of the Word which He gave, and through which He still works on human hearts. This is a great mistake and the prolific parent of all kinds of evil. Directly we put aside the Word of God, we lay ourselves open to the solicitation of the many voices that speak within our hearts; and we have no test, no criterion of truth, no standard of appeal. How can we know the Spirit of God in some of the more intricate cases which are brought into the court of conscience, unless our judgment is deeply imbued with the Word of God?

We must not be content with the Spirit without the Word, or with the Word without the Spirit. Our life must travel along these two, as the locomotive along the parallel rails. The Word is the chosen organ of the Spirit; and it is only by our devout contact with it that we shall be enabled to detect His voice. It is by the Word that the Spirit will enter our hearts, as the heart of the sun passes into our chambers with the beams of light that enter the open casement.

We need a widespread revival of Bible study. These mines of Scripture, lying beneath the surface, call loudly for investigation and discovery; and those who shall obey the appeal, and set themselves to the devout and laborious study of the inner meaning of the Word, shall be soon aware that they have received the filling that they seek.

There is no better way of communing with God than to walk to and fro in your room or in the open air, your Bible in hand, meditating on it and turning its precepts and promises into prayer. God walks in the glades of Scripture, as of old in those of Paradise.

BE PREPARED TO LET THE HOLY GHOST DO AS HE WILL WITH YOU

The Holy Ghost is in us, and by this means Christ is in us; for He dwells in us by the Spirit, as the sun dwells in the world by means of the atmosphere vibrating with waves of light. But *we must perpetually yield to Him, as water to the containing vessel.* This is not easy; indeed, it can only be accomplished by incessant self-judgment, and the perpetual mortification of our own self-life.

What is our position before God in this respect? We have chosen Jesus as our substitute; but have we also chosen Him by the Holy Spirit as our Life? Can we say, like the Apostle: *"Not I, but Christ liveth in me"?* If so, we must be prepared for all that it involves. We must be willing for the principle of the new life to grow at the expense of the *self-life.* We must consent for the one to increase, while the other decreases, through processes which are painful enough to the flesh. Nay, we must ourselves be

ever on the alert, hastening the processes of judgment, condemnation and crucifixion. We must keep
true in our allegiance to the least behest of the Holy
Spirit, though it cost tears of blood.

The perpetual filling of the Holy Spirit is only possible to those who obey Him, and who *obey Him in
all things*. There is nothing trivial in this life. By
the neglect of slight commands, a soul may speedily
get out of the sunlit circle and lose the gracious plenitude of Spirit-power. A look, a word, a refusal, may
suffice to grieve Him in ourselves, and to quench Him
in others. Count the cost; yet do not shrink back
afraid of what He may demand. He is the Spirit of
love; and He loves us too well to cause grief, unless
there is a reason, which we should approve, if we
knew as much as He.

RECEIVE HIM BY FAITH

"As ye have received Christ Jesus the Lord, so
walk ye in Him." Faith is the one law of the Divine
household. And as once you obtained forgiveness
and salvation by faith, so now claim and receive the
Holy Spirit's fullness.

Fulfill the conditions already named; wait quietly
but definitely before God in prayer, for He gives His
Holy Spirit *to them that ask Him;* then reverently ap-
propriate this glorious gift, and rise from your knees
and go on your way, reckoning that God has kept
His word, and that you are filled with the Spirit.
Trust Him day by day to fill you and keep you filled.

According to your faith, so shall it be done to you.

There may not be at first the sound of rushing wind, or the coronet of fire, or the sensible feeling of His presence. Do not look for these, any more than the young convert should look to feeling as an evidence of acceptance. But *believe,* in spite of feeling, that you are filled. Say over and over, *"I thank Thee, O my God, that Thou hast kept Thy word with me. I opened my mouth, and Thou hast filled it; though as yet, I am not aware of any special change."* And the feeling will sooner or later break in upon your consciousness, and you will rejoice with exceeding great joy; and all the fruits of the Spirit will begin to show themselves.

BUT REMEMBER IT IS NOT ENOUGH TO BE FILLED ONCE FOR ALL

Like the Apostles of old, we must seek perpetual refillings. They who were filled in the second chapter of Acts were filled again in the fourth. Happy is that man who never leaves his chamber in the morning without definitely seeking and receiving the plenitude of the Spirit! He shall be a proficient scholar in God's school, for the anointing which he has received, like fresh oil, shall abide in him, and teach him all things. Above all, he will be taught the secret of abiding fellowship with Christ, for it is written, *"As it hath taught you, ye shall abide in him."*—(1 John 2:27.)

Whenever you are conscious of leakage, when the exhaustion of service has been greater than the reception of fresh supplies, when some new avenue of ministry, or freshly discovered talent, or new department of your being has presented itself, go again to the same source for a refilling, a recharging with spiritual power, a re-anointing by the holy baptism.

Three tenses are used in the Acts of the Apostles of the filling of the Spirit, which have their counterparts still:—

Filled: a sudden decisive experience for a specific work (Acts 4:8).

Were filled: the imperfect tense, as though the blessed process were always going on (Acts 13:52).

Full: the adjective, indicating the perpetual experience (Acts 6:8).

There is, of course, more in the doctrine of the Holy Spirit than is at all realized by this writer. The fiery baptism of the Holy Spirit may be something far beyond. Let us not then be content to miss anything possible to redeemed men, but, leaving the things that are behind, let us press on to those before, striving to apprehend all for which we have been apprehended by Christ Jesus.

Moody Press, a ministry of the Moody Bible Institute, is designed for education, evangelization and edification. If we may assist you in knowing more about Christ and the Christian life, please write us without obligation to: Moody Press, c/o MLM, Chicago, Illinois 60610.

Printed in the United States of America